Praise for *Musical Theatre Acting*

"This is one of the most comprehensive handbooks on musical theatre performing I have come across in over a decade. Maybe two decades. JV has created a complex, layered, and shockingly user-friendly way to better oneself in this industry. . . . This is a 'read once a year' kind of book for any actor."
—**Alex Brightman**, two-time Tony Award-Nominated Actor (*School of Rock, Beetlejuice*)

"Muscular, empowering, and chock full of ways to learn to direct yourself, this essential resource gives those who pick it up the courage to trust themselves and their craft."
—**Kate Baldwin**, two-time Tony Award-Nominated Actress (*Finian's Rainbow, Hello, Dolly!*)

"With this excellent book, JV Mercanti gives the musical theatre actor a comprehensive, challenging, and completely practical way to not only do the work of acting in a musical but to kindle the spark of inspiration that makes magic onstage possible."
—**Michael Mayer**, Tony Award-Winning Director (*Spring Awakening*)

"JV Mercanti has written a most delightful book on how to be a thoughtful, grounded, smart, creative actor. Easy to read and completely compelling, it should be read by everyone in love with the theatre who wants to know more and be more.

JV truly knows his stuff and shares that wisdom with great humor and intelligence. Get into it!"
—**Emily Skinner**, Tony Award-Nominated Actress (*Side Show*)

"This is an incredibly important book—required reading for all young artists in pursuit of professional work in the musical theatre from a master teacher and director."
—**Erin Dilly**, Tony Award-Nominated Actress (*Chitty Chitty Bang Bang*)

"JV has written a book I wish I had had in my hands before entering the theatre industry. He clearly details the true work of an actor both in and outside of the rehearsal room, offering an approach that is both refreshingly practical (as promised) and surprisingly holistic."
—**Briga Heelan**, television and Broadway star (*Once Upon a One More Time*)

"A fiercely lucid guide to a life in the theatre. As luminously practical as it is wise. But what makes this book so special to me is the clear-eyed joy with which it expresses a love of the theatre as the study of life in all its strangeness, contradictions, and beauty."
—**David Leveaux**, director of *Jesus Christ Superstar Live in Concert*

"JV Mercanti's *Musical Theatre Acting: A Practical Guide* is an absolute essential for any actor, director, or theatre-maker at whatever stage in their career."
—**Chari Arespacochaga**, director and educator

MUSICAL THEATRE ACTING

A Practical Guide

JV MERCANTI

FOREWORD BY
JUSTIN GUARINI

APPLAUSE
THEATRE & CINEMA BOOKS

Bloomsbury Publishing Group, Inc.
ApplauseBooks.com

Distributed by NATIONAL BOOK NETWORK

Library of Congress Cataloging-in-Publication Data
Names: Mercanti, J. V. author. | Guarini, Justin, 1978- writer of foreword.
Title: Musical theatre acting: a practical guide / JV Mercanti; foreword by
   Justin Guarini.
Description: Essex, Connecticut: Applause Theatre and Cinema, 2024. |
Includes index. | Summary: "Musical Theatre Acting: A Practical Guide
   serves as a guide to the beginning musical theatre artist, the student, or
   the professional who needs a refresher on how to hone and sharpen their
   skills while honoring the material and their interpretation of it. Drawing
   on the teaching techniques of JV Mercanti, who has trained countless
   emerging performers in Pace University's acclaimed Musical Theatre
   program, it takes readers through a journey of mind, body, and spirit in
   order to engage the full self when it comes to creating a performance.
   Covering everything from script analysis and character research to
   auditions and rehearsals, this is a long-overdue roadmap for the performer
   who knows that success in musical theatre means a lot more than just
   singing well"—Provided by publisher.
Identifiers: LCCN 2024021958 (print) | LCCN 2024021959 (ebook) |
   ISBN 9781493077427 (paperback) | ISBN 9781493077434 (epub)
Subjects: LCSH: Acting in musical theater.
Classification: LCC MT956 .M47 2024 (print) | LCC MT956 (ebook) |
   DDC 792.602/8—dc23/eng/20240513
LC record available at https://lccn.loc.gov/2024021958
LC ebook record available at https://lccn.loc.gov/2024021959

"Don't settle for mediocre. It's ok to fail, but only if you fail on your quest to becoming extraordinary."

—Bob Fosse

Contents

CONTENTS

CONTENTS

Foreword

Justin Guarini

"Fame is for suckers . . . "

This is one of the first things I tell my students and mention in my keynote presentations worldwide, as I introduce my audiences to the concept of *success in the entertainment business*.

I've experienced the blessing and the curse of performing live in front of thirty million television viewers night after night, participating in seven Broadway shows, reaching hundreds of millions through a seven-year national soda commercial campaign, being interviewed by Oprah, and interviewing some of Hollywood's biggest names.

Curse? The "been there, done that, hope you think I'm cool" list above is certainly a blessing (for which I am grateful), encompassing every success and failure I've experienced in this business. However, the real curse was how long it took me to understand that fame and fortune weren't my true goal.

At age twenty-two, when most performers are just beginning to navigate the thrilling uncertainties of the entertainment industry, I was strapped to a metaphorical rocket ship—the first season of *American Idol*—hurtling into a different dimension at six million miles an hour, clinging on for dear life. What I didn't realize at the time was that the entertainment business—that I thought would lovingly embrace me and take care of me if I worked hard enough for it—was less like heaven, and more like Las Vegas.

If you've ever been to Las Vegas, you'll understand my analogy. The commercials show people having fun, slot machines dinging, people dancing, and an air of youth and beauty everywhere. There's excitement around every corner, and it seems like you can't lose just by being there.

Upon arrival, you're hit with all that glorious excitement, entertainment, and youthful energy. You're entranced by and revel in it, and it feels wonderful. The next day, however, you find yourself a bit poorer. But hey, you're in Vegas! So, you go out again, party more, spend more, win a little but lose more. This cycle continues until, by the third or fourth day, the magic has faded. You're tired, possibly hungover, with less money and energy than when you arrived. All you want then is to return home, to normalcy.

That's what this business can be like over the decades it takes to "make it," even for the most successful entertainers, if they pursue a career or remain in the industry *solely for fame and fortune.* We've seen it repeatedly, decade after decade: bright entertainment stars shining with intense brilliance, then suddenly extinguishing. Perhaps you can recall a star who developed harmful habits, went broke, or lost their life while coping with an industry designed to lure you in, chew you up, spit you out, and replace you with someone younger and more attractive.

The good news is *this does not have to be your journey.*

In my twenty-three years of high-level experience in the entertainment business, I have been blessed to encounter and learn from some of the greatest mentors, friends, and fellow stars in the business. I'm proud to call JV Mercanti a dear friend and mentor, which is why I'm so excited that he finally wrote this book.

In your hands is an instructive and insightful book for those passionate about musical theater (people like you and me!). I've known JV for a long time and have had the greater pleasure of working with him and being directed by him in two Broadway shows. I can say with certainty that he knows his stuff: he talks the talk and walks the walk. In this book, you'll discover his personal journey from passionate theatergoer to successful Broadway director, and through his eyes understand the importance of embracing self-belief, authenticity, and trusting in your unique abilities and instincts.

Professionally, you'll appreciate that JV is an exceptional director who has studied under other great directors and understands the casting process with an intimacy few achieve. If your passion for musical theater prioritizes impact and fulfillment over fame and fortune, then this book is for you. JV reveals the key qualities essential to becoming a great performer and guides you to realize your true potential.

As if that weren't enough of a service (I wish this book existed twenty-three years ago), you'll also find vital answers to significant challenges performers face in script analysis and character development. It offers practical tips and strategies you can apply today to achieve your musical theater dreams. *Musical Theatre Acting: A Practical Guide* is a thorough and motivational resource for actors at all career stages, emphasizing self-awareness, diligence, and deep craft understanding. I couldn't be prouder to endorse and celebrate my friend for this significant achievement and contribution to our community.

If there's anything I've learned about the entertainment business, it is the cyclical nature of its existence. If you are kind to people, do good work, and never give up on yourself, opportunities for you to shine and become the performer you were meant to be will keep coming around and around and around to you. This book is one of those opportunities. It's here for you to discover how to make an impact and find fulfillment in a well-lived life and a well-loved career.

Overture

"We owe it to each other to tell stories."

—Neil Gaiman

I

I saw my first Broadway show when I was ten years old. My family, spearheaded by my cousin Vinny and his partner Gene, would rent a bus and we would head from Philadelphia to New York City for the day. While my aunts passed out homemade pepper and egg sandwiches, Vinny would sing showtunes on the driver's microphone, breaking into "The Best of Times" from *La Cage aux Folles* when we entered the Lincoln Tunnel.

That spring of 1985, my first musical was *Singin' in the Rain*. I would only find out later that it was based on a famous Gene Kelly movie. As we walked into the Gershwin Theatre, I was immediately struck by the grand staircases and the sheer volume of marble. Being a good Catholic boy at the time, I knew that this was a sacred space. The only other place I knew with this much marble and grandeur, after all, was a church. Marble was for altars.

I was shocked by the noisy buzz of the patrons in the lobby. Weren't we supposed to be hushed? The buzz grew louder and louder as we mounted the stairs and reached its peak when we entered the huge auditorium. These people were excited to be here. The sense of anticipation was huge.

The lights began to dim. The overture began (does anyone still write an overture?) and the audience quieted down. My heart was in my throat. The rest of the world began to fade away and this ten-year-old boy was transported away from the real world of school, homework, bullies, and chores into a magical land where anything was possible. Just when I thought the experience couldn't get any more intense, the leading man (Don Correia playing Don Lockwood) was left alone on stage, the lights focused in on him, and he began singing. Then he began dancing. Then the stage very slowly began to move and tilt upward. And it began to rain. All of these elements came together to create a perfect theatrical moment. There was no one else in the theatre but Don Lockwood and me. Nothing between me in the mezzanine and this person so perfectly embodying the character on that huge stage. There was a cut to black, followed by thunderous applause. The lights slowly came up in the auditorium. And, like I was slowly waking from a dream, I had tears in my eyes.

My parents assured me the show wasn't over. This was just intermission—a break. Then there would be more!

After the show, merchandise in hand, we boarded the bus to head to dinner. Everyone knew it was my first show and all I wanted was to talk about it. Suddenly someone shouted, "There they are!" I pressed my face to the bus window to see two of the leads (the aforementioned Don Correia and leading lady Mary D'Arcy) walking down Eighth Avenue. They were normal people . . . but what they'd just done was superhuman! The bus driver honked. We waved our Playbills, and they stopped and waved back. Then they were gone, swallowed by the post-matinee crowds. I did not yet realize they would have to do it all over again that evening.

I was hooked. I inhaled musicals, plays, classic movies, movie musicals, books, everything I could get my hands on. The family trips continued once a year into high school. Then we added a December trip with just my parents and me. I would see every touring production that came through Philadelphia. Theatre was not only my escape, it was my passion.

II

I was in shows in high school. I took private voice lessons at Philadelphia's Settlement Music School. I collected cast recordings, learning as much as I could about the art form, but

I didn't have any structured musical theatre training. I decided to change that by attending New York University. I knew that I needed to be in New York City. My world exploded. I could see a show almost any day of the week: at school, on Broadway, off-Broadway, in Brooklyn. The city was bursting with theatre. I also learned I could "second-act" shows: walk in at intermission to shows I'd already seen, grab an empty seat, and see the second act for free! And I could study, learn, practice, and observe.

I began to take theatre history classes, literature classes, writing classes. I started to learn how works were properly structured—and when they were not. I took acting and directing classes, practical classes that allowed me to *do*. My objective was to make theatre and surround myself with people making theatre. I studied with incredible and not-so-incredible instructors, but I learned from both kinds. I was acting a lot, but I always felt as if I were standing outside myself while performing—watching and judging, but never inhabiting my character. Then I discovered directing and realized I was *never* outside of my body. I was fully engaged at all times when working, never second-guessing myself. I had found my lane and pursued it fully. I took all I knew about performing, literature, music, and history and channeled that into my directing work. Acting and directing are so closely linked in my mind, heart, and history that I can no longer separate the two. Acting is what led me to directing.

Then something magical happened. I was working in the NYU Office of Career Services as part of my work-study arrangement. It was a tedious office job. I spent hours inputting internship and job postings into the weekly newsletter for student access. One September day, I came across a posting for a casting internship at Roundabout Theatre Company. I had recently seen their revival of Stephen Sondheim's gem *Company*. I didn't know much about casting. But I knew I wanted to be in the business, and I knew I had a lot to learn, so why not work somewhere where I would be in the middle of it? I stealthily put the internship posting in my bag without entering the information into the newsletter and I applied myself. Two days later I had scheduled an interview. Three days later I got the gig. Six months later, two months before graduation, I was hired as a full-time casting assistant and my career in New York theatre had begun.

Talk about "the room where it happens": I was in the room with Sam Mendes and Rob Marshall as they began to conceive their Tony Award–winning production of *Cabaret* starring Alan Cumming and Natasha Richardson. I spent a Saturday afternoon in the theatre with Arthur Miller as Michael Mayer auditioned actors for his stunning revival of *A*

View from the Bridge. I listened. I observed. I provided input. I had a voice in the room. And I had the unparalleled pleasure of calling performers to offer them their first Broadway role. I hadn't even been working for a year.

That first year in casting, which I spent in audition rooms almost daily, was a life-changing education. I witnessed actors at all levels of experience auditioning for musicals and plays, both classic and contemporary. I began to define for myself what I considered a great actor:

A great actor understands the story they're telling.

A great actor has an emotional connection to the material.

A great actor brings their own unique persona to the role.

A great actor defines the character's objective and pursues it fully.

A great actor has an idea about the character and the skills to make them come alive.

A great actor is passionate.

A great actor understands physical space—their own and that around them—and uses it to their advantage.

A great actor knows how to modulate their voice to keep the listener engaged.

A great actor knows that their greatest asset is their partner and plays off of them.

A great actor is active, always fighting for their life.

A great actor is present, listening, fully engaged, and alive.

A great actor finds joy in everything they do.

That first year I also realized what was missing from even the best actor training. Performers would come into the audition room and have no storytelling abilities. They weren't aiming for an objective. They were sometimes not in control of their emotional connection to the material—or worse, they had no connection. They would stand in the center of the room and belt their audition cut with no sense of dynamics. If they had a side (an excerpt from the script), they wouldn't engage with the reader (the person hired to act with the auditioner). Some thought making choices meant making an impression, not honoring the material.

What is a "choice?" A choice happens when you've made decisions about a character based on your knowledge, understanding, and interpretation of the text. You understand who they are and what their objective—what they want—is. You understand the circumstances they are in. You have an emotional connection to the material. You are active and alive. You're playful, even when it's dramatic work—and by "playful" I mean taking in your partner, saying "yes" to what they're giving you, and responding to that one hundred percent.

I remember that, during the casting for the 1997 revival of *Cabaret*, a gentleman came in, pulled off his pants to display boxers covered in red hearts, put on a tacky blond wig, and looked us dead in the eyes and said, "There's going to be drag in it, right?" He then started playing the worst trombone I've ever heard. A few bars in the music director whispered, "It's the theme to *The Flintstones.*" And, indeed, it was. And, indeed, we all got the worst case of the giggles we've ever had in a professional situation. This wasn't storytelling; this was . . . well, I don't know what it was, other than memorable.

Conversely, Brittany Murphy—one of the stars of the hit feature film *Clueless*, which had just opened—gave the freshest, most truthful, and alive audition for *A View from the Bridge*. She took my breath away. She was incapable of dishonesty; her face was a mirror to her thoughts and emotions.

My career since that first year has taken many different paths, but the spine that holds it all together is my pursuit, admiration, and championship of great acting. As a director, casting director, and teacher, it's what I'm most passionate about and what drives me. I sit in so many audition rooms and watch actors scared or unable to make choices, actors who don't understand the story they're telling, actors who have no emotional connection to the work they're interpreting, actors who are waiting to be told what to do and how to do it.

Ultimately, actors need to be such amazing storytellers that they can, in essence, direct themselves. It is my hope that through this book and sharing with you the tools I've accumulated in over twenty-five years as a casting director, associate director, graduate student, director, producing associate, professor, and superfan that you'll be able to accomplish this. You'll be the performer who reaches that ten-year-old in the audience wherever you're performing and light the fire that will blaze in them for the rest of their life.

III

Acting is hard. Some people will tell you otherwise. They're wrong. Our ultimate goal as performers is an active simplicity with moment-to-moment truthfulness. That's difficult enough to achieve in our daily lives, let alone on a stage, with lines, music notes, and choreography, under hot lights, wearing heavy costumes, in front of hundreds or thousands of strangers. It's your job to make it look easy. In my experience, it takes a lot of work and practice to make things look easy.

Musical theatre acting is an Olympian endeavor. You will need to employ every ounce of your physical, mental, psychological, emotional, and spiritual energy in order to perform and stay in peak condition. This is the reason so many performers have little social life outside of the theatre when in performance mode. They're resting and preparing for the marathon of an eight-show week on their one day off.

In theory, musical theatre acting isn't different from any other kind of acting. You're always searching for the truth of the moment. You want to honor what the writers have created while interpreting it through your unique individuality. You have to know the wants and needs of your character while also understanding the style, genre, and time period of the world of the show. What's different about musical theatre acting is that you have to incorporate it into your performance with choreography and music. I've found that most educators and directors of young people tend to focus on the music and choreographic aspects of the art form and neglect the acting portion.

What follows are some tips, tricks, and advice I've picked up over the years that I find invaluable and will give you, the performer, a solid foundation on which to build the rest of your performance. This is a piece of what I teach every year. Sometimes you'll need all of these tools; sometimes, just one or two. Hopefully, you'll practice these enough that, eventually, a lot of them will become second nature.

As a performer, you're the one who's out on stage every night. You're the one who's responsible for your choices. I want you to feel that you've done everything possible to create a three-dimensional, fully alive, unapologetic performance. No matter the direction or choreography, you're the one responsible for shaping what the audience sees. You have to own it. This work will help you direct yourself, because this isn't an art or a business where you can stand around waiting to be told what to do.

What do I mean by "direct yourself"? I want you to be able to make smart, thoughtful, and bold choices that are emotionally rich and serve the story. I want you to respond to the instincts of a character that, oftentimes, might be very different from your own. I want you to live in the moment-to-moment truth of the dramatic circumstances while being able to zoom out and see what the bigger story means for your character and their development.

I hope no matter where you are in your career, whether you're a beginner just discovering the theatre or a working professional, that you can read this book and deepen your practice. I take for granted some basic techniques you would learn in an introductory acting class, but this should help you on the road to script and score analysis and character development. I have tried to define those terms and phrases that need explaining, but if you come across something that you don't know the definition of, please look it up immediately. This is part of your work.

A warning: there is homework involved. I don't know any other way to put it. I don't know how to make it sound fun. I'm asking, nay, requiring you to sit down and put time, energy, and thought into what you're creating. It's time to stop flailing aimlessly as a performer or relying solely on instinct. That doesn't mean there's *not* fun to be had. Of course we want this to be fun. And I promise it will be. But it is *hard work*. Commit to it and put away what you don't need for another day. I promise you'll need it eventually.

Finally, it's important to keep this in mind: there is no magic pill. There's not one true method that will work for you. No process will ever be the same. Sometimes you'll have to employ all the tools in your belt and still need to find more inside of you. Sometimes it will feel like a cakewalk. Most importantly, don't stop learning. Performance skills require muscularity, and like all muscles they need attention, exercise, and rest. You should work and study with as many teachers as possible. Commit to what they're sharing for the duration of the time you're with them. When you've finished, keep what works and file away what doesn't—you might still need it one day. I bet you will. But don't reject the method until you've committed to it.

So, shut your phone off or put it on airplane mode and place it in another room. First, we need to focus. Let's get to work.

Act I

THE PERFORMER

"I am what I am, and what I am needs no excuses."

—Jerry Herman

You

It all begins and ends with you. You are enough. You are limited only by the borders of your imagination. I firmly believe that if you can imagine it, you can achieve it. Don't waste your time trying to be what you think other people want you to be. You'll drive yourself crazy.

You're unique.
You're weird.
You're talented.
You're wild.
You're wonderful.
It's all in you.

Don't put yourself in a box. Other people are going to spend the rest of your life trying to do that to you. Create the best, loving, most empathetic version of yourself that you can and want to be. Stay open. Stay vulnerable. Accept failure as part of the process. Stay resilient.

Trust yourself.
Trust your instincts.
Trust your talent.
Trust your skill.
Trust your work.
Don't let the voices of doubt overpower the voice of reason.

Don't succumb to suspicion of the people you're working with. You'll inhibit your process and the process of all your collaborators. I promise very few people are actively, intentionally working against you. We all have the same goal—to create a successful show.

Fear and Failure

When you start to accept that everyone in the room, from producer to production assistant, is as scared—and as excited—as you, you'll be great. We want to be perfect, and we know that we won't be, and this can paralyze us. The truth is, we practice an imperfect art form. Musical theatre is active, alive, and live. Something will go wrong. You will mess up. No one is going to be mad at you for trying. They will get frustrated if you don't try.

In high school, I was in a production of *West Side Story* at the sister school to my all-boy's Jesuit preparatory school, playing Big Deal, one of the Jets. I had a very short exchange stage left with Tony and was then supposed to run off stage right. I turned around, and as I was preparing to run, I noticed that one of the painted brick flats was beginning to fall. So, I ran really fast, and I caught it. I barely stopped moving as I continued off stage, flat in hand. Well, I thought I had saved the show but everyone in the audience started cracking up: they thought I had run into the flat and broken it. So, even when you do the right thing, it can still look wrong to an audience.

More than anyone else I know, musical theatre performers, especially at younger ages, suffer greatly from "I Want to Be Liked" syndrome. The root of this is in our perfectionist tendencies. There are "right" notes to hit. There are prescribed steps to execute. There is exact dialogue to say. And if you do those three things "correctly," the director will "like" you, and you'll be cast. The difficulty with ideas of "right" and "wrong," artistically speaking, is this: Who's the arbiter? You'll never get it "right" if you're constantly trying to please someone else. And if you're auditioning, you probably can't read the decision-makers' minds to know what they think is "right." You're fighting a losing battle and, most likely, defaulting to a "correct" but bland performance lacking in spontaneity, passion, and risk. Remember in the "Overture" when I said I was always on the outside looking down at myself as a young actor, judging the performance while it was happening? This was the perfectionist in me—the controller who was afraid to let go and actually play in the moment.

Sometimes we look around the room and jump right into comparison mode: that person is smarter, more attractive, more talented than I am. That's all subjective. The only thing they might be is better prepared than you. But we're here to fix that.

Remember: you were cast for a reason. Take your fear as a given and don't let it impede your process or the processes of those around you. Your fear, if it paralyzes you, can stop the entire production from moving forward. We're all in it together and your contribution is invaluable. If your desire is strong but your fear is impeding your development or performance, it would be helpful to talk that through with a professional. Many performers suffer from anxiety. You're not alone. Don't ignore it. Acknowledge it. Learn how to manage the anxiety as well as your own expectations.

Ultimately, if you believe that fear is directly linked to getting it "right," you probably also consider yourself a perfectionist. Perfectionism is boring. It's inhuman. We are inherently flawed beings. We go to the theatre to watch flawed characters make mistakes and succeed. We're most alive when the risk of failure is all around us. And when we're acting, that risk should be everywhere.

When I was the associate director on the national tour of *Cabaret*, we rehearsed the new cast members in New York City for a few weeks before joining the tour and putting them in with the members of the company who were staying on. One of the new actors going in was playing Fräulein Schneider, the owner of a boarding house in Berlin. Schneider has a very tense relationship with Fräulein Kost, one of her boarders, a "Kit Kat Girl" who brings various gentlemen back to her room, breaking the house rules.

While rehearsing in New York, the actor playing Schneider followed her impulses, and this led to some slight changes in the blocking of the scene. When we got to San Francisco to put her in, these staging changes totally derailed the actor playing Kost, because it changed the power dynamic that she had been used to playing every night. The actor playing Kost fought every change to the point that she was on the verge of tears. Her fear of change derailed her. It was very primal. It literally stopped her from experiencing what her new partner was giving her. It also showed very little grace to an incoming company member. The actor playing Kost completely shut down, and it took months for her to recover. All I could think was this: why practice a live art if you can't adjust to changes?

The quest for perfectionism can also paralyze us, stop us in our tracks, and cause us to procrastinate. It can be used as an excuse, a crutch, that keeps us from actually taking the risk. If we take the risk, we might expose ourselves and then fail.

Failure goes hand in hand with fear. We are afraid we will fail. Guess what? We will. I have failed at one time or another in all my roles. And when I fail, I fail big. That's a part of my process. I have to accept that and learn from it and not repeat the mistakes. I've taught myself to compare my work to a scientist in a lab. Scientists perform test after test, sometimes for years, failing on a daily basis. Then, one day, they have success. They need to try every option before landing on the one that works. Each failure has led them one step closer to success. Why do we think differently about that? Why is perfectionism somehow the median for our work? Accept fear and failure as part of your work without judgment.

Health

Your physical, mental, emotional, and spiritual health are of the utmost importance. Performing requires that you be open, flexible, and resilient in these areas. Make sure you have support in all of them. Again, this is an Olympian artform.

Discovering yoga changed my relationship to my body and my mind. Exploring the possibilities of how my body could (and couldn't) move forced me to be present in a way that could be unbearable at first. I had a great guide who taught me to distinguish between pain and discomfort. Pain means stop. Discomfort means you're changing. If it hurts, you stop. If it's uncomfortable, you stay with it for as long as you can. And you drop into child's pose and take a break when you need it. Most importantly, yoga taught me to breathe. I can't tell you how many times I would realize I was holding my breath, or not breathing deeply enough. Yoga made me conscious of this so I could recognize and fix it. This was invaluable.

Yoga led me to weight training, and through that I learned about my body and mind in a different way. At first, like many people, I was concerned with how I *looked*. But the more I practiced, my focus shifted to how I *felt*. It's a not-so-subtle distinction and one that took a long time to learn. In fact, I'm still learning it and that's okay.

I also go to therapy, not because there's something "wrong" with me, but because I need someone to help me recognize and break patterns of behavior that impede me from growing. Also, being an artist means I'm constantly exploring and utilizing my emotional life, and this can take a toll. It can bring up uncomfortable and scary thoughts and feelings. Having a professional assist in the management of this is invaluable. Friends are great for venting, but having someone more experienced and more objective to help navigate the roller coaster of this career and life has often been a necessity.

Try everything. Find what works for you. It might be religion, a place of worship. It might be a sport. It might be—as you can see it is with me—a combination of many things.

Don't be afraid to ask for help. Vulnerability is an asset, not a sign of weakness. Asking for help is not a sign of weakness. Ask your friends, mentors, teachers, and colleagues what they do to stay healthy in body, mind, and spirit. Try everything without judgment and discover what works for you.

Consent and Empowerment

You are your own best advocate. While I believe a musical theatre performer is there to serve the show, it should never be at risk of your own physical or emotional distress or harm. If you're in a professional, academic, or amateur environment, you should be familiar with systems in place to report potentially dangerous situations. Most likely, these will be explained on the first day of class or rehearsal. Whether they are or are not, here are some ways to proceed:

1. Communicate directly with the creative who is activating your discomfort. You can do so in the moment, on a break, or outside of rehearsal hours.

2. If the issue persists or for some reason you are uncomfortable speaking directly to the creative, speak with the stage manager. In an Equity show, you'll have an Equity deputy (a representative member of the company elected by the company to field issues) who can

advocate for you. In a college, university, or training program you should approach your program head, chair, or dean.

3. Consent needs to be given daily and can be revoked at any time. Whether you're working on a fight scene or a scene requiring intimacy, you are in charge of explaining where you're comfortable being touched and where you're not that day. Hopefully, your show will have fight and intimacy directors on the team to help you navigate these situations. If it does not, you need to be very explicit with your partner about touch.

Navigating these levels of discomfort can be challenging, but they are necessary in order to keep the work environment collaborative and creative. Ten minutes of awkwardness are better than eight or more weeks of repressing your needs and feelings. If systems of reporting are not in place, and you aren't in a position to help implement them, reconsider the gig.

Qualities

The following are some qualities that I believe make a great performer. They can all be nurtured and fed with time and practice. Some may come naturally; others may need encouragement. This is by no means a comprehensive list.

Clarity

You need to be coherent in what you do while performing. Making choices on stage doesn't mean guessing. It means committing to something clear and specific, based on your analysis of the text, and seeing if it works. The worst choice is no choice or an ambivalent one.

You also need clarity when speaking with your collaborators. "This doesn't work" simply isn't an appropriate response. If you flag an issue, you need to be able to clearly define it. You can try the following approaches:

"What I'm trying to achieve in this moment is ____."

"It would helpful here if I could ____."

"Can you explain to me what you're trying to achieve in this moment so I can help?"

Effective Collaboration

Egos are important, for sure, and we all have one. But you have, for better or worse, chosen a profession that demands working together. Musical theatre is a marriage of many different minds. Ultimately, the most important thing is the show. You are one piece of a very large (and, if it's Broadway, expensive) puzzle. Are the feelings you're feeling and the choices you're making about *you* or the *show*? Learn the difference and do everything you can in service to the show.

Openness to Feedback

One part of effective collaboration is the ability to take a note. Some people (present company included) can bristle when a note is given. Remember: notes are necessary. The person giving the note is seeing something you can't see because you're too close to it, or what you're doing lacks clarity from the perspective of the audience. Notes are given to enhance your work, not detract from it. Notes are not judgments. Listen to the note with grace and then spend some time thinking about what it means and how to implement it. It is your job to execute all of them, if given from the creative team. However, keep in mind the following:

Don't note your cast mates.
Don't ask for notes if you don't want them.
Don't offer notes if not asked.

I told you earlier that when I fail, I fail greatly. I once sent unsolicited notes to a former student I cared about deeply after seeing them perform. What I thought were a few help-ful points on strengthening their performance were not taken well—and were not mine to give, certainly not in that manner. Notes are personal. You don't know someone's process; and given at the wrong time, you can actively impede the work they're doing. Lesson learned—but learned the hard way.

Courage

Creating art is risky. It requires you to be vulnerable. So many people have the passion and the desire but not the courage to follow through. Or they make great choices while refusing to take in anyone else or anything in their environment, control-ling the outcome, too afraid of how they'll respond if they truly respond in the moment. Every time we create something we risk rejection. If your work reaches and moves even one person, you've done your job.

If you can't major in musical theatre or don't get accepted into a program, find another place to practice, whether in the form of voice lessons, acting classes, community theatre, or something else. The most important thing is that you don't ever let anyone tell you "you shouldn't" or, worse, "you can't." Listen to and trust yourself. Accept that fear is always a given, then have the courage to act. Even though I went to NYU for undergraduate studies, I didn't major in theatre. I designed my own course of studies through what was then the Gallatin School of Individualized Studies.

Creativity

Imagination and creativity are directly linked. If you have the ability to imagine something, you then need the tools and the bravery to execute it in reality. Artists should spend a lot of their time daydreaming about what they're working on.

When you have an idea about a character, a moment, anything—*do it*. Don't wait for, or ask for, permission. Creativity also means allowing your ideas to flow without judgment. Don't censor yourself. Don't listen to the voice in your head saying, "That's a bad idea." Creativity must constantly be fed and nurtured.

Creativity also is useful in periods when you're not working on a show. Can you create your own? Write a ten-minute play. Write a one-act play. Write a full-length play. Write your own musical. Create a web series. Even if no one but you ever sees it, make something.

Curiosity

Look around you. What interests you? Ask questions of your family, your friends, your teachers, your mentors. Ask them about their lives and their stories. How did they get to where they are? Listen to understand, not just to respond with a story of your own. Simply listen.

Watch strangers on the street, in a coffee shop, in restaurants, anywhere in public.

Watch how people behave when they don't think anyone is looking.

Play with an animal.

Play with a child.

Look at familiar surroundings with new eyes.

Go someplace you've never been and simply sit and take it in.

Go to a park and experience nature.

Go for a hike.

When you're doing eight shows a week, after a year can you still remain curious about your scene partner(s) and the circumstances of the story? The world is so interesting you should never be bored.

You love Sondheim? Can you find and listen to and watch everything he wrote? Read his books? You're an Audra McDonald superfan? Have you listened to all her recordings? Have you watched her film and television work? Did you know that Harvey Fierstein, James Earl Jones, Patti LuPone, Ethel Merman, and Elaine Stritch, among many others, have written memoirs about their lives in the theatre? Read them.

When I was in my first year at NYU, I didn't have Friday classes and I knew that the *amazing* New York Library of Performing Arts had a video library of recorded Broadway shows. Every week I would view a show that I was a fan of but never had the opportunity to see.

Earlier, I would sit in my high school library and read reviews of shows I had missed but loved listening to in order to see what others thought about them. What did they think worked about a show? What didn't? Why didn't they love this performance I couldn't get enough of?

Read books—fiction, nonfiction, graphic novels, newspapers. *Wicked* was adapted from the novel of the same name by Gregory Maguire. *Hairspray* was originally a 1988 film.

Go to museums. Did you know that George Seurat's 1896 painting "A Sunday on the Isle of La Grand Jatte" inspired Sondheim and Lapine to write the musical *Sunday in the Park with George*? Did you know that Bible stories inspired *Joseph and the Amazing Technicolor Dreamcoat, Jesus Christ Superstar,* and *Godspell,* among others?

Inspiration is all around you, but it doesn't magically appear. You have to search for it.

Dependability

People want to work with other people who they know are going to show up and do the work. For me, personally, being on time is late. I need a moment to arrive at work, adjust to my surroundings, and prepare myself—mentally and physically—for the day ahead. If my workday starts at 10 a.m., I'm often in the building, in the room, and preparing myself by 9:30. That half hour is invaluable to me. I need it.

Assume that in most professional settings you won't get a vocal and physical warm-up. If your day starts at 10 a.m., you need to be ready to work at 10 a.m. Show up on time. Have your music memorized as soon as possible. Unless someone tells you differently, have your lines memorized after the first time you've staged the scene. Run the choreography until you know it better than anyone else.

If you're passionate like I was, you'll sit in the room and watch the rehearsal even if you're not called. You'll listen to what the creative team is saying to other performers and learn how to filter that into your own work on the show. Everything you absorb will make you a better performer. Bottom line—you have to show up on time, you have to be ready to work, and you have to work.

Empathy

Sympathy is acknowledging the feelings of someone else. Empathy is actually understanding them. You can't perform a part if you don't have empathy for the character. If they do terrible things (Madame Morrible, for instance), it's not your place to judge them. You have to act them. If you're judging them, you're not allowing yourself to inhabit them. The truth is people do terrible things, sometimes intentionally and sometimes not. Conversely, it's just as dangerous to judge a character in solely positive terms.

Sutton Foster got the character of Millie Dillmount to explode on stage not just because of her joy but because of her faults: stubborn, clumsy, and short-sighted. She embraced the positive and negative aspects of the character. If our job is to shine our light on all of humanity, then we need to explore the good, the bad, and the ugly. Even if you're playing the leading character, find their faults, their mysteries, and their hubris. We all have them.

Energy

As human beings, we are constantly managing our relationship to energy: we are energy, we give energy, we receive energy, we exchange energy, and we block energy. In our personal lives, we're usually adjusting this, consciously or unconsciously. For example, when we're with someone we love, we open ourselves up to be in a free exchange. Conversely, when we're on the subway and someone is acting loud or threatening, we try to turn ourselves off, make ourselves smaller so as to not emit energy and be seen.

When in rehearsal and performance mode, you need to allow yourself to be open to both giving and receiving energy. This exchange between you and the company and you and the audience has to be constant. You want the audience to leave with more energy than they came in with. This exchange requires supreme vulnerability and, as most performers are empathetic, this might take a toll on you. Knowing how to rest, recuperate, and recharge is integral. I'm sure you've seen performances where an actor is exhibiting too much or too little energy, and it's disappointed you. I worked with a young actor many years ago who was playing a moody, introverted character, and all of his energy was directed inward. He was the lead, but he became a black hole. No one could get into him, and he gave nothing off. There was no exchange. It caused a huge imbalance and, ultimately, from the perspective of the audience, he disappeared while everyone else on stage rose above him.

Focus

Can you do all of the above unplugged? Can you leave your phone off or at home? Can you keep the earbuds in your bag? Can you be present and focused and observe what's going on without any other sound? Can you trust yourself and the silence and allow your mind to wander, roam, and search? If you go to a museum and discover a painting you love, how long does it keep your interest? How long can you read without checking your phone?

If you're doing eight shows a week for over a year, can you keep yourself alive and focused on your partner(s) in the moment and not rely on muscle memory or, worse, go on autopilot? I once had a very talented student who was on the road with *Jersey Boys* for over a year. He called me while on the road to say that he found himself, during a performance, tuned out and staring at the tie clip of a castmate during a scene. He was on autopilot. Then he heard my voice in his head challenging him to listen, really listen. And he found renewed vigor and energy in his performance. He found the desire to go on stage every night and discover something new. This was one of the best phone calls I've ever received.

Intelligence

Oh, I'm not talking about being book smart. I don't care what your GPA is, nor will anyone who you're auditioning for. (I do want you to have script analysis and comprehension skills—that's a big part of what this book is all about.) I want you to be *emotionally* intelligent. Have you ever been in an argument and thought, I should walk away right now because I'll say something hurtful if I don't? That's emotional intelligence. Knowing when not to send the reactive text or email—that is intelligence.

Emotional intelligence comes down to vulnerability, taking the focus off yourself and directing it to those around you and your environment. It's an extension of empathy. It requires focus. It requires trust—understanding that people most likely aren't out to hurt you, they're there to serve the show.

It means being curious about those around you.

It's about listening, knowing when to speak and when not to.

It can be about anticipating the needs of those around you.

It's about knowing when and how to give a note and when not to.

It means recognizing that the people around you are all going through something you don't know anything about and giving them a little grace.

It means accepting that some choices have to get made without your input and moving on without holding a grudge.

It means dealing face-to-face with a problem and not allowing it to fester or, worse, explode.

Emotional intelligence requires the ability to zoom out, see the bigger picture, and realize it's not always about you. Therapy is a great place to develop and hone this particular quality.

Imagination

I was a reader from a very young age. I still love getting lost in stories. I also was something of an outcast, so I would often spend hours in my house staging incredible adventure stories and romances with my action figures. My imagination was my best friend. I found that, the older I got and the more the "real world" crept in, my imagination became something that needed to be fostered and nurtured. There are assignments to turn in, bills to pay, survival jobs, emergencies, and suddenly, your imaginative life is neglected. Acting, directing, reading, films, and television all helped me return to that world. If I can see it in my mind's eye, it becomes real. Visit museums, go to a concert, read history, and expand your world. Exercise your curiosity and your imagination will bloom.

Joy

Joy, for me, is the most attractive quality in a person. You can do the work, you can take it seriously, but if you enjoy the work and enjoy the storytelling, then I'm immediately engaged with you. Storytelling is sharing. Take joy in sharing your talents and skills with an audience, even in an audition situation. Sometimes auditioning is your one opportunity to perform that week. Embrace it.

Passion

If you're reading this book, you *love* musical theatre. I love musical theatre. I discovered it when I was ten years old, and there's been no turning back. I can (and often do) talk about it all day long. But here's a thought: nurture other passions—drawing, cooking, baking, sports, gardening, knitting, and so on. We all need a break from what we love sometimes. Don't judge others for their passions. Share your passion but know when to back off.

Persistence and Patience

Some people around you are going to find success seemingly overnight. Some will find it late in life. Some never will. Remember that we're all on our own paths and you have to be wary of judging others and judging yourself. You shouldn't "be" anywhere than where you are at any given time. And no one deserves success more than anyone else. Don't expect this to be a fair industry. It just isn't.

Playfulness

If you can read all of the above and still think "that sounds like fun; I want to do that!" then that's the right attitude. Having a sense of play is necessary for this profession and requires so many of the qualities outlined above: curiosity, imagination, creativity, courage, openness to collaboration, and energy! When we play, we tend to say "yes" more often than not. Playing means accepting what you're given from your collaborators and going with it, without judgment. This is the basis of "Yes, and . . . ": you take what you're given, accept it, and expand upon it.

Directly tied into this is the concept of "positive choices." A positive choice is a "yes, and." A negative choice is one in which you're constantly shooting down everything being thrown your way. You're blocking, not listening, not playing. You can always make choices to defend yourself, but it has to be an active choice. (I'll explore this later on in the "Actions" section.) A negative choice shuts you and your partner down, leaving one or both of you stranded. It kills the energy. A positive choice doesn't mean a "happy" choice. It means an engaged, active choice.

Problem Solving

Before you've flagged an issue or asked someone else to fix a problem, is there anything you can do to fix it? You don't have to announce it. You don't have to let anyone know you did it. Just do it. Move a prop that needs it. Fix a traffic pattern that's wonky. (But do not give notes to other actors, ever!) If you can't fix it yourself, go to the creative team or stage manager. I've had many actors in rehearsal come to me with a helpful suggestion that required giving another performer a note. I gave the note, and the problem was solved. This is the appropriate way to proceed.

Stamina

Musical theatre is an Olympic sport—I can't say it enough—but your career span is much, much longer than an athlete's. It requires all your physical, mental, emotional, psychological, and spiritual energy. That means being and staying healthy. It also means knowing when to rest. We are not machines.

Uniqueness

There is not another you! Even if you're a twin, you're unique. Embrace that. Accept yourself in all your weirdness, your perceived imperfections. That's what's going to make you interesting. Don't try to be what you *think* other people want you to be. That's an endless loop. The most popular musical theatre stars are different, slightly off, interesting because of their oddities. They are nonconforming. Why shouldn't you be you?

Vulnerability

An open mind and an open heart are our most important assets. If we're not open, we won't channel energy from our partners or our inspiration. Balancing the world and remaining vulnerable in your life and work is a constant struggle, but it's worth it. As I noted in the "Health" section, it takes great self-awareness to learn when we need to protect ourselves and when (and how) we need to allow ourselves to be vulnerable. This can sometimes feel like a business in which people are constantly telling you "no." Holding on to the reasons why you do it requires strength and vulnerability. The two go hand in hand.

As I said, this is but a short list of the qualities I look for in performers, collaborators, and in myself. I believe there's a way to practice building, strengthening, and nurturing all of them. It's worth evaluating your experience on a regular basis to see how you're exercising these qualities—or, if you're not, how to engage them. When you're feeling uninspired or, worse, bored, can you practice any of the above, get off your phone, and get out in the world?

Actor Consciousness vs. Character Consciousness

All of the text that follows this section is focused on helping you, the performer, understand how to use the script and score to your advantage as a storyteller. Great storytellers understand every aspect of the narrative. They know it so well that they're able to live and breathe inside the story while telling it. There's no guessing involved. You, the actor, need to know every detail so that your character can be blissfully ignorant. Also, I want you to know the text and music even better than your director so that you can, in fact, direct yourself.

I was once directing a production of *Floyd Collins*. Everything was going really well except for one scene that, no matter how many times we rehearsed it, just wasn't working. In the scene, Skeets Miller, a journalist, is the only person who can physically get down the tunnel to the trapped Collins because of his slight stature. He attempts to dig Floyd out.

I had two highly skilled actors, but no matter what adjustments I gave, the scene would not come to life. I finally threw my hands up in frustration and said, "This isn't working and I don't know how to fix it!" Then the actor playing Skeets said something very telling. He said, "Well, I don't see the point. I know that I can't get him out." And I paused. Then I prodded: "You know you can't?" He said, "Well, I know that I don't." Aha! Actor consciousness vs. character consciousness. I said, "Can we do it again, and you believe that you are going to be able to dig him out and the story will be over?" And we did. And all of a sudden, the scene finally came alive.

The actor knows he doesn't free Floyd, but the character has to believe he can!

Exploring and Breaking the Barriers: Binaries, Bodies, Disabilities, and Race

Musical theatre is still catching up to the recognitions, changes, and advancements happening in the above categories. Certainly, Golden Age material is usually built around outdated perceptions of society, culture, sexuality, politics, identity, and so on. I do not believe that means we have to throw away the entire canon. Instead, we can challenge, reexamine, and reinvent the material, viewing it in a different light, in a different era. Daniel Fish's award-winning revival of *Oklahoma!* is testament to that. He cast a woman of color (Rebecca Naomi Jones) as Laurie and a woman in a wheelchair (Ali Stoker) as Ado Annie but made no changes to the book or lyrics. These characters were simply portrayed as written in the script and each audience member was allowed to interpret the portrayals on their own.

If you identify as trans or nonbinary, please don't let that stop you from bringing your own unique point of view and life experience to these (or any) works. Don't feel like you need to compromise yourself in order to fit into these worlds. Imagine how exciting it would be to present nonbinary representation in something as "traditional" as *The Pajama Game*, or something classic but still daring like in the role of Sally Bowles in *Cabaret*. It's our job as artists to reflect the world back at itself. Trans and nonbinary peoples have existed throughout history, and we can bring those stories to light in these works while, hopefully, new works will reflect those experiences in a clearer and more nuanced light.

If you're a person of color, show the auditioner what your Cliff Bradshaw or Sally Bowles reveals about World War II Germany. While these musicals are historical, they are by no means accurate "history." Theatre has never been and never will be literal, as Diane Paulus's revival of *1776* and Lin-Manuel Miranda's *Hamilton* have proved! Literalism is boring. People don't burst into song and dance in real life, so we've already thrown convention away when we enter the theatre.

To this day I can think of only three musicals in which plus-size women were the leads: *Hairspray*, *Head Over Heels*, and *It Shoulda Been You*. Why? This is by no means a reflection of the world we live in, and yet the "leading" physical stereotypes exist. This must change. You can make that change happen. Can Elphaba not be in a wheelchair because Nessa is? Or Jesus or Judas? Javert or Valjean? This is me telling you not to settle. "It's always been this way" has never been a good excuse.

Once, I was directing a studio production at Pace University. There had been a number of graduating seniors who hadn't had, in my mind, sufficient performing experience and I wanted to do something for them. At Pace, we pride ourselves on our diverse student body. I really wanted to direct *Angels in America, Part One: Millenium Approaches.* The play means a lot to me, personally, and it's so nonliteral that I thought it would hold up well with little to no design support.

I called up a friend who was intimately involved in the initial development of the play and asked if it was a show that could be cast with a diverse group of actors. He thought about it and then said, "You know, I don't think it can. The race, ethnicity, and religion of these characters is part of what defines them." And I thanked him. And I thought about it. And then I thought, "JV. Why are you being so fucking literal?! You love theatre because it is universal."

So I cast the best actors for the parts. And we spent four weeks discovering *their* versions of those amazingly rich, complex, and flawed characters based on their experiences and interpretations. To this day it remains one of my most cherished theatrical experiences and it reinforced for me *why* I do theatre: to tell stories. And to stop being so fucking literal.

You know and I know that it's not your job to educate anyone about your journey. You can, however, challenge the industry's perceptions and invite theatremakers to see their work in a different light. In any case, find and work with the people who want to break the barriers with you. And prove the nay-sayers wrong. For an art form that depends on imagination, you're going to find many—especially those in charge—who have little of it. The industry will change and that change starts with you.

Conclusion

I want you to know as much about yourself as possible because you, after all, are your own instrument, and it's for life. I want you to learn how to function comfortably within the perceived limitations of your body, mind, and spirit and then push against those limitations to expand your own boundaries. The more you know about yourself the more adept you will be at inhabiting the bodies, minds, and spirits of other people.

Act II

THE BOOK

"All the best performers bring to their role something more, something different than what the author put on paper. That's what makes theatre live. That's why it persists."

—Stephen Sondheim

Introduction to the Five Reads

I am obsessed with hearing actors speak about their process. It's safe to say that, over the years, I've read and watched hundreds of interviews with actors. Upon being asked how they prepare for a role, the actor inevitably responds, "I read the script. Then I read it again. Everything I need to know is in there." And the answer appeases the interviewer who then moves on to other questions. But I'm left wondering: How do you read the script? What do you look for? How do you gather and collate information? Do you simply hope for inspiration to strike? What clues are you looking for? So, I set about finding a way to teach the actor how to read the script as a detective, mining it for facts, questions, and clues that will allow them to read with intention. I want you to know the script and your character so well that you can direct yourself.

I'm asking you to read the script five times with a certain objective on each read-through. Hopefully, you'll read it more than five times, but this is a structured start. These will be thorough reads. I urge you to silence your phone and, better yet, put it in another room. Grab a notebook and pen or pencil. I recommend, if you're able, that all your notes, thoughts, ideas, and work be done by hand. There is a connection when we write by longhand—from the fingers to the heart to the mind—that facilitates the absorption and retention of information in a way vastly different from the sometimes-mindless action of typing or texting. All your work from here on out needs to be intentional, from reading to writing to interpreting to action. That being said, if it's necessary for you to use an electronic device to do your work then go for it, but do it mindfully—and with airplane mode activated.

Here's a quick breakdown of the five reads:

1. General Read
2. Facts and Questions
3. Everything I Say about Myself
4. Everything I Say about Other People
5. Everything Others Say about Me

I will go into detail about these in the coming sections. But, before we move on, let me briefly touch upon two concepts that will be important for your reads: story structure and the writer's intention.

Story Structure

Remember, as a storyteller it is imperative that you can recognize some basic points about narrative and structure. Even in abstract or nonlinear works, you should be able to define these elements. This is part of an actor's job. It is not only the responsibility of the writer, director, or dramaturge.

The Status Quo

The world as it exists when the lights come up. The so-called normal world of the protagonist.

Inciting Incident

The event that sets the story in motion and activates the protagonist to action.

Rising Action

The protagonist pursues their objective and faces numerous tests and obstacles along the way.

Climax

The highest point of action, when the protagonist stands at a crossroad and must make a life-altering decision.

Resolution

The protagonist has achieved their objective (or not) and is victorious or transfigured in some way.

The Writer's Intention

The writer's intention is their purpose, their reason for writing the story—to educate, to entertain, to instigate, to question, to trouble. It may be a combination of all these. Every good writer will have a purpose and, better, a clear, strong point of view.

Hairspray is about the joy, the power, and the necessity of integration.

Spring Awakening is a warning to adults in power about the dangers of withholding information from young people.

Hadestown is about the power of love and how, no matter how dangerous, it's worth pursuing.

Fiddler on the Roof is about the strength and resilience of tradition and community.

Sunday in the Park with George is about the necessity of creating new art.

Wicked is about accepting and owning your identity.

Some questions that will help you decipher the intent:

- What are the major themes of the work?
- Who is the main character?
- What is their objective?
- Do they win or lose?
- What is the style, tone, and genre of the piece?

The Five Reads

1. The General Read

Pour a beverage, grab a snack, and find a comfortable seat. I would love you to do this reading in one sitting. If you have to break this reading up and the show has two acts, try to do an entire act at a time. I want you to, quite simply, read the script. Let the story wash over you. See the big picture. Don't focus on your part. Don't count your lines. Experience the work as a whole.

Then grab your notebook and answer these questions:

- How/what did the work make you feel?
- What moments/images from the text stand out?
- Who is the main character?
- Can you briefly define their journey? What do they want? How do they finish versus how do they start? How has the status quo changed after the resolution?
- What are the themes of the work—major and minor?

- What is the inciting incident?
- What is the main event of act 1?
- What is the main event of act 2?
- What is the climax of the show?
- What doesn't make sense to you?
- What do you think the writer's intention is?
- What other thoughts or responses or questions do you have?

It's really important that you don't edit or censor yourself during this part of the process. No one is reading or seeing this save for you. Your initial responses are important. If you want to write down "red" or "pink" or "paisley" or "plaid" because that's how the work made you feel but you don't know why, that's okay. Write it down. You don't have to know what it means. But you might be in rehearsal one day, be stuck on a moment, and think to yourself that the moment is "pink." And that might mean something to you that puts moments, songs, or scenes into focus. The mind, like art, isn't always literal.

2. Facts and Questions

This read-through takes a lot of time. I would suggest you not try it in one sitting. It's almost impossible. Grab your notebook, pen, beverage, snack, and find a comfortable seat: here we go!

Read through the script as if for the first time. Even though you have prior knowledge of the work from the first reading, I want you to divorce yourself from that knowledge and write everything down as it's revealed to you.

As you read through, you're going to make two running lists in your notebook: one of indisputable facts and one of all the questions you have.

An *indisputable fact* is any piece of information that cannot be questioned or challenged. If you're playing Moritz Stiefel in *Spring Awakening*, for example, your first fact would be "My name is Mortitz Stiefel." There's no basis on which to question this.

Your running list of *questions* would be about character history, relationships, the world of the play, and so on. As you read, some of your questions will begin to be answered by the text. Therefore, you can cross off the question on that list and transfer the information to your facts list.

It's important to know that your list of questions will be longer than your list of facts—and it should be! We make lots of assumptions when we read, and this exercise is designed specifically to stop you from making those assumptions before investigating more deeply. I want you to be the most curious about the character you'll be playing. In this exercise, it's almost like you and the character are going on a series of dates, and you want to know everything you possibly can about them. This is where you fall in love with them.

Why do we do this? Most beginning acting classes are designed to help you open up, follow your impulses, and respond instinctively to the stimuli around you. This is necessary. Hopefully it breaks through some of the learned behaviors you've cultivated that cause you to censor yourself from responding truthfully to the stimuli around you. When creating a character, however, you need to respond not as *you* but as *them*, with their impulses, their history, and their knowledge. In this exercise, you begin the process of getting to know them as well as you know yourself so that you can respond *as* them.

WARNING: There's a fine line between thinking and overthinking this exercise. I'm not asking you to question or challenge everything. If your character is a known liar (like Iago from *Othello*) don't wring yourself out trying to prove them otherwise. Finally, do not censor or edit yourself. Write down anything and everything that you want.

The following is an example of "Facts and Questions" for the character of Moritz Steifel in *Spring Awakening,* reading through from the top of the show up to the song "It's the Bitch of Living." That is about five and a half pages of script. In my notebook, I suggest doing *Facts* along the left-hand page and *Questions* along the right-hand page so you can reference each easily.

MORITZ STIEFEL / *SPRING AWAKENING*

Facts	Questions
My name is Moritz Stiefel.	What was life like in 1891?
The year is 1891.	How old am I?
I live in provincial Germany.	What kind of house do I live in?
I am in class.	Do I have siblings?
We are called upon to recite out loud from Virgil's Aeneid.	Are both my parents alive?
There are only boys in class.	Do they work?
Herr Sonnestich is the teacher.	Can women work in this time period?
Otto is a student.	What does "provincial" mean?
Georg is a student.	What is Virgil's *Aeneid* about?
Hanschen is a student.	When was it written?
Ernst is a student.	Do I like it?

Facts	Questions
I am asleep in class.	What language is this?
Melchior is a student.	Is school segregated by gender?
Melchior defends me.	Is there a completely separate school for girls?
Melchior gets hit for defending me.	How do I feel about the other boys?
We sing a song.	Who am I closest to? Why?
The music is contemporary, electronic.	Who do I not like? Why?
Melchi becomes a rock star and we're his backup.	Why am I asleep?
I call him Melchi.	Does this happen a lot?
I thank Melchi.	What time of day is it?
I didn't sleep all night.	What season is it?
I suffered a visit from the most horrific, dark phantasm . . . a nightmare. Legs in blue stockings, climbing over the lecture podium.	Why are there so many ellipses in my dialogue?
I call this a mortifying vision.	Why do I not respond to Sonnestich?

Facts	Questions
I find out Otto had a dream like this about his mother.	Am I scared of him?
Georg had a dream like this about his piano teacher, Fräulein Grossbustenhalter.	Do I respect him?
Sonnestich grabs my ear and tells me that, of all the students, I'm not one to be taking liberties.	Am I like this in all my classes?
	What's it like to be bored in class?
	Have I been hit before? By teachers? At home?
	Do we always break into song like this?
	Is this new?
	Do I study? Do I do my homework?
	How often do I have dreams like this?
	Is this nightmare a sex dream?

Facts	Questions
	Am I afraid of sex?
	Am I ashamed of how I feel and what I think?
	Do we have sex ed?
	Have my parents told me about sex?
	Am I a virgin?
	Have I ever seen another person naked?
	Does everyone tell Melchi their dreams? Why?
	How long have I known Melchi? Since we were little?
	Is Frau G my piano teacher too?
	Can women work other than teaching?
	Am I musical?
	Is this a public or private school?
	Do my parents have money?
	Are we religious? What kind?

This is so much to question and I'm not even through act 1. But a great detective asks questions and loves it. This part of the homework is often my favorite. It really focuses me and allows me to play the role of detective for my own character. I can remain outside of the character but completely engaged.

As you answer your questions, you can cross them off your list. You will always have a list of questions remaining that are not answered in the text. Once you've finished your five reads you can begin to make educated, informed inferences from your accrued knowledge.

3. Everything I Say about Myself

Read through from start to finish as if you've never read the script before and write down everything you say about yourself. Writing the complete line is very helpful.

Don't cheat! Read the whole play. Don't skip to your scenes. Don't look specifically for the self-referential lines. With this exercise you're starting to build your point of view about yourself—how you see yourself.

The following is an example of some things the character Usher says about himself in Michael R. Jackson's *A Strange Loop*. The huge amount of information below is from the opening number alone!

USHER / *A STRANGE LOOP*

Everything I Say about Myself

Pg. 12: In the background, there will be a young over-weight-to-obese homosexual and/or gay and/or queer, cisgender male, able-bodied university-and-graduate-school-educated, musical-theater-writing, Disney-ushering, broke-ass middle-class far-Left-leaning Black-identified-and-classified American descendant of slaves full of self-conscious femme energy and who thinks he's probably a verse bottom but not totally certain of that, obsessing over the latest draft of his self-referential musical *A Strange Loop*! And surrounded by his extremely obnoxious Thoughts!

Pg. 13: He wants to show what it's like to live up here and travel the world in a fat, black queer body.

Pg. 14: He has to fight for his right to live in a world that chews up and spits out black queers on the daily.

Pg. 15: He tries to scramble and dodge or extricate, but still his fate lies in wait like a scavenging vulture.

Pg. 16: All he wants is to subvert expectations, black and white from the left and the right for the good of the culture.

Pg. 18: I am a Disney usher. I'm barely scraping by. My discontentment comes in many shapes and sizes, but I woke up this morning and I told myself to try. I told myself that I would make no compromises.

Pg. 19: I smell awful 'cause there's no time to shower. I plaster on a smile, pretend I have no brain. Make nice with asshole tourists hour after hour. . . . Today I plan to change my whole life forever.

Pg. 20: I want to break the cycle that's so ingrained in me, but change comes way too slow. And I am in a hurry. There's all of this rejection, which brings such misery, but with my white girl music I drown out the flurry of today.

Pg. 20: So days like this just get me. I hate days like today when I see myself and see the same reflection. Someone who's stuck rewriting but stuck in his own way. Someone who plans to edit every imperfection. Today I plan to change my self.

This exercise is really important because sometimes we say things about ourselves that aren't true, or that we want to be true, or that we want others to think are true. We can be defined by the things we say about ourselves. Here we start to decipher the difference between what our character says and what they do.

4. Everything I Say about Other People

Again, the goal is a complete read-through, this time making note of anything you say about other people, whether they make an appearance in the show or not. With this exercise, you're starting to build your point of view about the people around you.

The following are some things Audrey says about other characters in *Little Shop of Horrors*. In this instance it's helpful to create a column for each character so you can reference them easily.

AUDREY / *LITTLE SHOP OF HORRORS:* OTHER PEOPLE

Seymour

Oh, we're just friends. I could never be Seymour's girl.

I don't even deserve a sweet, considerate, suddenly successful guy like Seymour.

Seymour's the greatest.

Seymour's a cutie. Well, if not, he's got inner beauty, and I dream of a place where we can be together at last.

Sweet little guy.

Orin

He's a professional.

> He's a rebel . . . but makes good money and, besides, he's
> the only fella I got.
>
> He'd get angry. And if he does this to me when he *likes*
> me, imagine what he'd do if he ever got mad.
>
> A semi-sadist.

Audrey 2

> Strange and interesting new plant.
>
> Exotic plants.
>
> Isn't that bizarre?
>
> Re: Audrey 2 " . . . after me?"

What we say about other people says just as much about their character as it does ours.

5. Everything Others Say about Me

On this final read-through, your goal is to look for anything other characters say about you. With this exercise, you're defining how other people view you. Sometimes the way we feel about ourselves and the way we present ourselves can be diametrically opposed. This can help clarify that tension.

Here are some of the things other characters say about George in *Sunday in the Park with George*.

GEORGE / *SUNDAY IN THE PARK*: THINGS PEOPLE SAY ABOUT ME

Dot

They were talking about you at La Coupole. Saying strange things . . . Were you at zoo, George? Drawing the monkey cages? They said they saw you.

Why is it you always get to sit in the shade . . . ?

He always does this.

That's you, George, you're bizarre. Fixed. Cold.

And, George, you're good. You're really good.

George's stroke is tender, George's touch is pure.

I love your eyes / beard / body, George. I love your painting.

The ground could open, he would still say "please."

Never know with you, George. Who could know with you?

George taught me all about concentration. "The art of being still."

George likes to be alone.

Sometimes he will work all night long painting. . . . George doesn't need as much sleep as everyone else. And he never tells me his dreams.

George has many secrets.

George is very special.

George could look forever. As if he sees you and he doesn't all at once. What is he thinking about when he looks like that?

It's warm and soft inside his eyes. He burns you with his eyes . . . But he's never really there.

Jules/Yvonne

Re: My work, "Une Baignade Asnieres."

No presence, passion, life.

Mechanical, methodical, drab, cold.

He's young but aging.

All mind, no heart.

How others see us is incredibly important. They might see something in us that we don't recognize. They might say something about how we carry ourselves, speak, or behave that we're not conscious of. This exercise helps you define how others see you within the world of the show.

Featured Roles and Ensemble Work

You can (and should) do this work even if you're cast in a featured role or as part of the ensemble. You are an integral part of the storytelling in these roles and need to know as much about the world of the show as everyone else.

There might be no contextual clues to help you define your character, but you can look to the music, the lyrics, the location, the time period, and so on. This probably means your list of questions will far outnumber your facts. Great! I love that. Here are some questions to consider:

- What am I singing about?
- What's the style of the music?
- What time period does the show take place in?
- What are the job options for me in this time period?
- What is my level of education?
- What is my current housing situation?

- What is my romantic life like?
- What is your social circle?
- Is my character here to support or challenge the protagonist?

Let's take a look at the some of the ensemble lyrics in "Put on Your Sunday Clothes" from Jerry Herman's *Hello, Dolly!* They read, in part, as follows:

Put on your Sunday clothes . . .
Strut down the street and have your picture took.
Dressed like a dream your spirits seem to turn about.

Here's a small sample of helpful facts from reading the play:

HELLO, DOLLY!

Facts	Questions
The action takes place in the 1890s.	How far is Yonkers from NYC?
The location is Yonkers, New York, and Manhattan.	Do I know Dolly? Do I know of Dolly?
Dolly Levi Gallagher is a widow and a matchmaker—the main and secondary plots are all about marriage. She likes to "meddle."	How much does she charge for her service?

Facts	Questions
Horace Vandergelder is a successful and rich business owner in Yonkers.	Am I married?
He has two employees.	Am I in love?
They take the train from Yonkers to Manhattan.	Do I know Vandergelder?
	When were cameras invented?
	Do I go to church?
	Do I work 6 days a week?
	What's my job?
	How much do I make?
	Who is my family?
	Where do I live?
	How much does it cost to live there?
	Do I have roommates? A partner?

Thematically, *Hello, Dolly!* is about people taking chances—whether it's Irene Molloy looking for her second love or Cornelius Hackl finding his first love. When the show is at its best, it feels like a shot of pure joy. This particular ensemble number functions as a parade of beauty.

In order for there to be joy, there needs to be sorrow. The very first line addresses this: "Put on your Sunday clothes when you feel down and out." "Down and out" implies that you're feeling sad, despondent, or even destitute. Therefore, you're dressing up to make yourself feel better. What happened to make you feel that way?

The next line is "Strut down the street and have your picture took." The camera is a relatively new invention in this time period. Getting your picture taken would be quite an experience!

The lines after that state that dressing nicely will improve your mood. We're back to the question of why your mood needs improving. Lost job? Lost love? Lack of money? Lack of love? Are you "strutting" to find a mate?

You can then track your way through the rest of the show like this until you create a path for your character that is both fun to play and has a journey.

I don't believe that members of the ensemble should "blend in." It's not your job as a performer to default to a neutral state. By doing this work and creating a character, you allow your own unique voice and personality to shine through. A great ensemble is one in which the performers build a vivid, diverse community while executing the same choreography. You are part of that.

Swings and Understudies

Yes, you have to do this work for every character you cover! It's not just about knowing the blocking. You have to know the character inside and out.

It is very important when in these positions to understand that you're walking a fine line between imitation and originality. When you're a swing or an understudy and you go on, you're slotting into a finely tuned machine. You want to be aware of the rhythm of that machine and try to stay true to that while finding space to play. Remember your fellow performers, musicians, stage management, and the crew are all waiting for certain cues: a prop move, a vocal inflection, a musical button. It's not your job to rebrand a character when you go on.

In rehearsal, it's your job to listen to everything the directing and choreographic team are saying to everyone about everything. This will help you find your own way into the character(s) while honoring the vision of the creative team.

Beyond the Five Reads

All this homework is to train you to be a detective. You're poring through the material so many times, with a different goal each time, mining it for clues. Once you have all the facts, you can start making informed deductions instead of generalized assumptions. Very few of us are trained psychologists (I'm not), but this detective work can help us put together a profile of our character through which we can begin to define and create behavior based on the facts. I find putting my "detective hat" on, as opposed to my "homework hat," to do this work makes it infinitely more interesting and fun.

The "five reads" are just the beginning of your work, though! You can and must dig even deeper and get more specific with your relationship to the show and your character. The following exercises will help allow you to do that while also helping you answer more of the questions on your list.

Abstraction and Images

At this point in the process, you might be tired from thinking so literally. I know I am. Here's where I like to go back to my themes and my "Facts and Questions" and start searching for images that inspire me based on that information. From there I create an image/vision/mood board (or Pinterest page) for the character/show. It's amazing and inspiring to find photos, paintings, art, architecture, and so on, that help bring you into the world of the show.

Objectives

An objective is, quite simply, what you want: your goal.

There are three types of objectives:

1) Super objective: This is what you want before the action of the show even starts and carries you through to the end. It never changes. You either win or lose.

2) Scene objective: This is what you want in each and every scene, based on your super objective. You enter into a scene wanting something and by the end you've either won or lost it. Either way, you have to work harder in the next scene to keep what you've won or make up for what you've lost.

3) Song objective: This is the reason you're singing the song. What are you trying to uncover/reveal?

The phrasing of an objective is simple and clear:

I want to [active verb, e.g., "find love"] or else
[undesired outcome, e.g., "I'll die alone"].

Your super objective is something you can whisper to yourself right before you go onstage that makes your eyes light up, brings you alive emotionally, and, energetically, brings you onto the balls of your feet. Your super objective is your fight! Your reason for living!

We don't go to the theatre to see victims. We go to see fighters. And, although the leading character might lose, we find empathy in their fight. This is why it's very important that we put an active verb after the "I want." You want to stay away from passive "to be" verbs here. Close your eyes and think: "I want to be loved." Okay. You did it. You felt something: loss, hope, loneliness, longing, emptiness. I bet physically you even sank into yourself a little when you thought it. But what did you *do* about it? Nothing. You sat in the feeling. You became a victim. So boring! Imagine two and a half hours of that! We all want to be loved but what are we *doing* about it? Acting is active.

In order to start defining your super objective, let's go back to your responses from your first, general read. I believe that all the clues to help you define the objective are in here.

For example, if I was preparing for the role of Tracy Turnblad in *Hairspray,* some of my initial responses to would be as follows:

Dancing	Racism	Mean Girls	Stereotypes
Body image	Biases	Activism	What is beauty?
Segregation	Class/Elitism	Love	Magic
Integration	High School	Rock & Roll	Prison
1960s	Music	Assimilation	Mothers/Daughters
Civil Rights	Entitlement	Appropriation	Drag

To craft the objective, I like to start with the "or else" half of the statement. This is our greatest fear. The "if I don't accomplish my goal this will happen" consequence. We're all going to die, obviously. Some people are afraid of that, some aren't. But when crafting the super objective, we need to be more specific than "or else I'll die."

Ultimately, Tracy's journey becomes about integration. She learns to look beyond herself. That leads me to believe that segregation could be her greatest fear—oppositions. She also finds her greatest joy in dancing. So, maybe, a stab at her super objective would be this:

> *I want to dance down all the barriers or else segregation wins.*
>
> or
>
> *I want to dance with all my friends or else the world won't see us as equals.*

Maybe too cerebral? Close your eyes and say them to yourself. Do they excite you? Do they change your energy? Do they make your blood rush? Do you inflate or deflate? What about this:

I want to dance for equality or else the "mean girls" win.

That's simple and playable. In this phrasing, "mean girls" incorporates racists, segregationists, and all the people that want to hold Tracy and her friends back. You're putting the super objective into Tracy's words as influenced by the world of the show.

Defining your super objective can be tricky, and it's something you're going to want to play around with and massage for a long time, especially during a long run—sometimes even until closing!

Scene objectives are short and practical:

I want to win a spot on the Corny Collins Show.

Easy. Relatable. Playable. The scene objective is determined by the "given circumstances" I'll discuss in the next section.

Finally, your song objective is immediate. In "Mama, I'm a Big Girl Now," Tracy wants to get permission to audition for the *Corny Collins Show.*

Given Circumstances

The *given circumstances* are the conditions that immediately influence the character. They answer three questions:

1. Who am I? Name, age, profession, class, and so forth.
2. Where am I? Country, state, city, street, building, room, and so on. May also answer questions like these: Where am I coming from? Where am I going? What just happened?
3. When am I? Season, year, month, day, time.

Unless the show takes place in one extended scene and one location, it's important to keep track of these changes as you go through the show. It's also important to start developing a point of view about these circumstances.

If your character is in their house, for instance, you might want to take a moment before labeling that place "home." In *Into the Woods,* "home" means something different to Cinderella than it does to the Baker and the Baker's Wife. Cinderella is now a servant in her home. She is not loved or cared for. It's a place that provides shelter but very little comfort. All traces of her previous life there have been erased by her stepmother and stepsisters. Conversely, the Baker lives in the house he was raised in. This place is not only his home but his business. It is where he hopes to raise his family, should he and his wife bear a child.

The woods for Cinderella contain the grave of her mother. They hold a place of reverence and possibility. She also feels safe there. The woods are more "home" to Cinderella than her house. After being visited by The Witch, though, the woods represent danger and the unknown for the Baker and the Baker's Wife.

You'll start creating substitutions for these locations so that your behavior, when you're performing, will reflect how you act when you feel safe or scared, or threatened, and so on. What place feels like a home to you—a place in which you're safe, warm, comfortable, and cared for? What place feels dangerous and unknown, but very real? For example, my apartment is my home. The ocean terrifies me. I would begin to play with these as substitutions. Going into the woods would be akin to scuba diving to me—I can't swim!

You would then do the same work with "When am I?" How does your character behave at 5 a.m. versus 5 p.m.? Personally, I love the peace and quiet of the morning and long walks with my dog; the solitude appeals to me. The hour of 5 p.m. on a noisy, crowded, hot subway car during rush hour in the summer might be one of the worst experiences in the world. All of the circumstances influence your experience.

Season is very important to consider. We behave differently in summer than in winter. You feel differently when dressed in multiple layers than you do in shorts and a T-shirt. Clothes affect how you move, how you hold yourself, how you move through the world. Outside, in the winter, we tend to close our body off to all the elements, collapsing our head into our chests against the wind, the cold, and the snow. In early summer you might find your gait a little more free and easy, your face turning toward the sun. In the late summer, you might find it impossible to move because the heat is so oppressive. You must be specific in all choices. And if your director doesn't make a decision, it's up to you to create the circumstances on your own.

All of these circumstances fuel how you feel, how you behave, and how you respond to everything around you. *Given circumstances* can also reveal polarities. At the beginning of *Into the Woods*, Cinderella is a servant in her father's house. At the top of act 2, she's princess of a kingdom. By the end of the play, she gives up her crown. Yet, she still doesn't feel at home in either. It's not until the end of the musical when she decides to live with the Baker and his son that she begins to think she's found a home. What a journey!

As you go through the script scene by scene, it's helpful to know where you're coming from, where you're going, what your expectation is going into the scene, and what has happened in the time between the current scene and the one before it. How has that period of time passing affected your character and their wants/needs/sense of urgency? How does your accumulation of experience help mold your relationship to the circumstances?

If you were playing Dot in *Sunday in the Park with George*, here's a look at the given circumstances for the first two scenes:

SUNDAY IN THE PARK WITH GEORGE / GIVEN CIRCUMSTANCES: DOT

Act 1, Sc. 1

1. Who am I?

Dot, 20s, model, working class, French, uneducated, mistress of George.

2. Where am I?

Paris, France, Le Grande Jatte, an island in the Seine River.

George and I took the 7:30–8 a.m. ferry (I slept on the half-hour ride) over to take advantage of the morning light. I am posing as George sketches me for a big painting he's working on. I am wearing a new dress, popular in style, that has a bustle, a corset, and petticoats. I am sweating. George gives me poses and I follow them. I do not know how long this sketching session will last. It's a long time to stand. Also, the sun is blazing. I am looking at the water.

3. When am I?

Summer, 1884, July/August, Sunday, anywhere between 8:15–10 a.m.

Act 1, Sc. 2

1. Who am I?

Dot, 20s, model, working class, French, uneducated, mistress of George.

2. Where am I?

Paris, France, George's Studio, sitting at my vanity, which is cluttered with make-up, perfumes, and other objects I love. I took the ferry back by myself because George stayed on the island to sketch. I probably ate something and took a nap. I am getting ready for the Follies. I had my first successful posing session with George today. He taught me how to concentrate. I have shed my hot, heavy dress. Nothing is fitting me right (I don't know I'm pregnant yet, but how far along am I?). My reward for being a good model is a trip to the Follies. I am very excited. I like to dream.

3. When am I?

Summer, 1884, July/August, Sunday, evening.

This exercise helps you put together a picture of your character's daily life. You'll find yourself adding to your "Facts and Questions" and "Research" lists as you do this exercise. Try to keep the given circumstances focused on facts, but you can start to embellish your point of view on the circumstances as well as make choices about what you did in the intervening time.

For example, Dot sings of sleeping on the ferry in *Sunday in the Park with George*, so I made an assumption that she sleeps on the way back as well. This is reinforced when she sings in "Color and Light" about loving to sleep and dream. Also, in "Color and Light" she speaks of her clothes not fitting right. We find out later in the show that she is pregnant. It's safe to assume that her clothes are not fitting her here because of the pregnancy but she's not aware of it yet. The actor would need to do some research on signs and symptoms of pregnancy and how it affects the body.

This work is less linear and more cyclical, with each assignment feeding the other, forcing you to think harder and more deeply about your work.

The World of the Show

Along with the given circumstances, the world of the show—meaning the boundaries and possibilities of the action contained within—is dictated by the genre, style, and tone. Examples include the following:

Genre: tragedy, comedy, drama, melodrama
Style: satire, naturalism, realism, rock, fantasy, pop
Tone: the point of view the writers have about the piece. Is it acerbic, amused, playful, serious, ardent, caustic, frank, ironic, and so on?

This might sound obvious to you, but think about it: Elphaba from *Wicked* could never walk into the world of *Spring Awakening*, even though they're ostensibly both musicals about teenagers coming to terms with who they are. *Wicked* is a magical world, inhabited by people, animals, a cross between the two, munchkins, and other assorted fantastical creatures.

Spring Awakening has a more realistic cast of characters, but they pull microphones out of their clothes and belt rock songs in heightened situations.

Even though both shows are written by the same composer, Bobby from *Company* couldn't appear in *Into the Woods*. Bobby (or, Bobbie, in the more recent gender-swapped version) inhabits the world of 1970s New York. Bobby/Bobbie's "woods" are dates. Stephen Sondheim writes not only to the world but to the character. If you listen, he will help you decode the world in which your character lives. There is a grandness to the music of *Into the Woods*, containing rich and fantastical sounds. *Company* sounds crowded, sometimes frantic: the sound of New York City. The wit of the characters is what unites them as Sondheim characters. The style of music helps dictate not only the mood of the piece, but how you perform it. "No One is Alone" and "Being Alive" hold the same space in the structure of the shows, but they have completely different sounds, styles, and meanings. By defining the world of the play, you're defining the rules and norms in which your character can perform in.

The character of Cinderella has been written by Rodgers and Hammerstein, Sondheim and Lapine, and Andrew Lloyd Webber and David Zippel, and depicted through the music of Britney Spears. She has to be portrayed differently in each of these versions because, even though her world is similar in each piece, the genre, style, and tone are completely different!

Lin-Manuel Miranda wrote both *In the Heights* and *Hamilton*, but those worlds are completely separate, even if they sometimes share the same sound, musically. If Usnavi, who runs a bodega in Washington Heights, walked into the New York City of 1776, we would laugh.

Main Event

The main event is something that happens—a moment, a decision, a change—that affects all characters on stage at the time, making the next scene necessary. Every scene will have a main event. Every song will have a main event. And every act will have a main event.

Of course, there will be many moments in a scene in which your character learns something and changes. These are events for your character but not necessarily the main event. The main event is the one that propels you to take the next big step. In a scene or song, you want to delay this moment for as long as possible. A simple example is entrances and exits. These immediately affect everyone on stage, even if they're done in secret.

For example, in *Les Miserables*, Fantine losing her job is a main event. Fantine doesn't go into work that morning knowing she'll get into a fight or be fired. Losing her job affects not only her but her coworkers (they are now responsible for making up her share of the work), her employer (he's responsible for the net product), and Valjean (he does nothing, and this will haunt him later)—everyone involved in that scene. Losing her job propels Fantine to sing "I Dreamed a Dream" and to sell her locket, her hair, and, eventually, her body.

Valjean lifting the runaway cart later in the show is another example of a main event. He does not know going into the scene that he can or will do this. But his feat of strength impresses the townspeople, giving them a story to tell for weeks, and clues Javert into who Valjean really is, propelling the next scene and, in fact, the rest of the story.

Christine making the decision to step through the mirror in *Phantom of the Opera* is another example of a main event. The Phantom is desperately in love with her. He needs her, but he needs her in his own domain. The only way he can get Christine to go is to scare her. Christine doesn't come into her dressing room knowing that this strange, deformed man is going to change her life. But when she makes the decision to step through that mirror, both their lives change forever.

Some main events are subtle and difficult to decipher. In the very first scene of *Spring Awakening*, Wendla's "Mama!"

that leads into "Mama Who Bore Me" is a main event, not only because it leads her to the song, but it signifies Wendla standing up to her mother and demanding to be heard and told the truth. George telling Dot they'll go to the Follies at the very end of the first scene in *Sunday in the Park with George* is the main event. Dot is seeking some form of validation and connection with George, and he offers it to her. In the next scene, we find Dot preparing for an evening out and George painting, knowing he's supposed to take her but unable to pull away from his work. At the end of that scene, George chooses the painting over Dot, and she storms out.

Notice that the main event is usually toward the end of the scene, giving you as an actor something to fight for the entire time you're on stage. Usually, the main character of the show is making the consequential decision in each scene that causes the action to move forward. In *Sunday in the Park*, it's George. In an ensemble piece like *Spring Awakening*, it is sometimes Wendla, sometimes Melchior, sometimes Moritz. It depends on who is on stage at the moment.

Similarities and Differences

What do you have in common with the character you're playing? Make a list. Now put that list aside. You don't have to work on any of those qualities. They're in you!

What are the differences between you and the character? Make a list. Here's where you want to spend your time thinking, daydreaming, and researching. This is your homework.

If I was to take on the role of George in *Sunday in the Park with George*, my lists would look something like this:

SUNDAY IN THE PARK WITH GEORGE: GEORGE

Similarities	Differences
We're visual artists. He creates images on canvas; me, on stage.	He is a painter, practicing pointillism.
Our work is sometimes solitary and sometimes collaborative but always involves other people.	He is twenty-five years old at the beginning of the show.
We live in large, metropolitan cities.	He knows a lot about color and light.
We are both logical.	I don't know how to sketch or paint.
We wake up early.	He is mathematically precise.
He is "teaching" Dot. I am a teacher. We can both be stern.	Paris in 1880s is very different from contemporary NYC.

Similarities	Differences
We like to be alone.	He seems to lack empathy in his single-mindedness.
Sometimes very close to his mother.	He doesn't seem to care what people say about him behind his back.
We talk to ourselves.	He has a scientific mind.
We're intense.	He makes promises he doesn't keep (because he gets caught up in work).
We have vivid imaginations.	He'll stay up all night painting. I like to sleep and dream, like Dot.
We can be playful.	Seems to have a strained relationship with his father.
We can be very cold when someone hurts us.	Only seems present when working.
We find it difficult to express our feelings.	Not very successful with relationships of any kind—intimacy issues?

The more you work on the character, the more each list will grow. You may find surprising aspects to both. Many of the items on this list will bleed over into your research. This work will also most likely influence your "Facts and Questions" lists, adding to each.

The overthinkers and procrastinators out there are going to want to spend time dwelling on the similarities—don't do it!

Relationships and Point of View

We have relationships with everyone and everything we interact with in our lives. It's rare that these relationships lack specificity. As an actor, it's your job to specify your relationship to all people, locations, costumes, and props you come into contact with over the course of the action.

If you're playing Louise in *Gypsy*, it's not enough for you to define your relationship with Rose as "mother." That is your biological relationship, yes, but it doesn't necessarily allow you to feel anything for her. Some people love their mothers; others, not so much. You might want to try defining her as your "god." A god is someone we fear, obey, want to please, and worship. Imagine how that would affect your behavior whenever you come into contact with her. And the immense courage it takes to stand up to her at the end of the show when you've come into your own power.

June is more than your sister. Again, that's simply biology. If she's a "shooting star," though, she's blazing, fierce, unstoppable, and out of your reach. By creating points of view like these, you're helping to further isolate Louise, and so when she's given the lamb on her birthday, she'll cling to it even more. The lamb is something that needs her, for once. It is something within her reach that she can hold on to.

These relationships and points of view extend to everything around us. I have a favorite pen, a preferred notebook, and a spot I like to write in. I have clothes I wear when I'm feeling good about myself and clothes I wear when I want to be comfortable. You do as well. So should your character.

Actions

Actions are, in many ways, the heart and soul of your work—and the hardest part. Actions are designed to get you out of your head, put your focus on your partner, and make certain you're making specific and active choices. Much like you chose an active verb for your objective, I'm going to ask you to choose an active verb for each and every line of dialogue and lyric you have. It looks like this:

I [active verb] you.

These verbs are meant to shape what you're doing to achieve your objective and how you're doing it. Actions also prevent you from simply playing the mood of the scene, relying on a generalized emotional state. Yes, you need to be fully emotionally alive when you're on stage, but then you need to do something with that life. Actions force you into contact with your partner.

You want to action every complete thought. That is any sentence ending with a period, a question mark, or an exclamation point. For example, if your line is

"Do you want a cup of coffee?"

in its simplest form you could render it as

"I question you."

Yes, for sure. But the fact that it's a question is implicit in the fact that the sentence ends in a question mark. So, unfortunately, "I question you" is too simple an action. It doesn't give your partner anything to respond to emotionally. Your action reflects your objective, your given circumstances, and your relationship to your partner.

Therefore, a line as seemingly innocuous as "Do you want a cup of coffee?" can immediately transform if you assign an action such as

"I seduce you."

"I threaten you."

"I cajole you."

"I reassure you."

"I comfort you."

"I test you."

What do you want? What are you doing to get it? How can this person help you? How you choose to play the action (comforting, cajoling, seducing, etc.) will define who your character is.

Is your character confident, scared, arrogant, anxious? Your actions will reflect this.

Put this into practice:

1. Say the line without any intention: "Do you want a cup of coffee?"
2. Now say the action and then the line: "I seduce you. Do you want a cup of coffee?"
3. Finally, take the action away but say the line with the intention still suffusing it.

I want you to think one thought, one breath. Don't break up the line of thought. Get from the first word of a sentence to the last in one breath, playing one action. Performers love to break up the thought of a line or lyric for no reason. When you act one thought and one breath, we call it acting "on the line." When you break the thought up you fall "off the line." For example, "Do you want a cup of coffee?" is one thought. Some actors will manipulate the line or break it up to make it seem more interesting (or, honestly, just to be different) when what they are doing is, in fact, confusing the intention. They'll say the line like this, for example:

"Do you . . . want . . . a cup of . . . coffee?"

Why? What does this do for you? It's infinitely more interesting to assign an action as spelled out above and play the action on the line! This can't be stated enough. Shows have a rhythm, a flow. If you're going to break that, do it with awareness and intention. Don't tell us how you feel; show us by how you're affecting those around you.

You might also be able to define your actions by asking: how do I want my partner to feel or respond? Deciding how you want them to feel might dictate what you're doing to them to get that response. "I want them to feel loved," so "I comfort you." Or, "I want you to know how much you hurt me," so "I accuse you."

Please don't confuse physical actions with intention. If your line is "Do you want a cup of coffee?" your action is *not* "I hold out a cup of coffee to you." That's blocking. There's a marked difference between physical action and intention!

However, metaphorically, you can play some physical actions as intentions:

"I slay you."

"I slap you."

"I cut you."

"I jab you."

Finally, there are incomplete thoughts. These might be lines or lyrics that end with an ellipsis (. . .) or a dash (—). Even these need actions, because they start with an intention. An ellipsis indicates an active thought in which you're searching for the next thing to say. It's not a stop! The energy continues as you search. A dash usually means someone, or something, has cut you off mid-thought.

Actioning is hard work and time-consuming. It forces you to sit down and really spend time with your lines and create a path of accountability and specificity.

Atmosphere

Every location has an atmosphere: physically, emotionally, spiritually, psychically. This atmosphere directly affects our behavior. People also tend to behave differently in private versus public. A place of worship feels different from a theatre, as I pointed out in the "Overture."

Walking into a room in which two people are having an argument has a very specific atmosphere. You most likely behave differently in your bedroom than you do in a coffee shop, or a classroom, or a library. You might behave differently on a first date than you do a year or five into a relationship. Your character will as well, and this behavior helps shape and define who they are.

The atmosphere of the flower shop in *Little Shop of Horrors* changes depending on the circumstances, and the songs reflect this. It's a sad, run-down place at the beginning of the show ("Skid Row"). The growth of Audrey 2 gives the place a new life ("Closed for Renovations"). Finally, it becomes a place of terror ("Sominex/Suppertime II"). The atmosphere changes whether Mushnik is in the shop or not. Other characters can have an effect on atmosphere.

The streets of Baltimore in *Hairspray* have a different atmosphere in "Welcome to the 60s" than they do in "I Know Where I've Been." The streets that provided a full makeover in act 1 now provide a place of reflection on the struggle for equality.

The stairs of the Paris Opera House in *Phantom of the Opera* are a site of celebration at the top of act 2 with the number "Masquerade," but that quickly turns to fear when the Phantom magically appears.

In *The Last Five Years*, Jamie sings "Nobody Needs to Know" to his new lover while they're in bed. If this is, in fact, his marriage bed, the atmosphere is shaken by there being another woman there who is not his wife.

The Moment Before

The "moment before" is what happens immediately before you step on stage, or begin a scene, and how it makes you feel. Millie gets off the bus in New York City at the beginning of *Thoroughly Modern Millie*, followed by "Not for the Life of Me." Your *moment before* would literally be stepping off the bus, defined by the fear and the excitement of starting a new life in a big city.

Audrey misses Seymour's first radio broadcast because of a violent encounter with the Dentist in *Little Shop of Horrors*. Those incidents, along with the probing questions of the Urchins, make "Somewhere That's Green" necessary. Your moment before might be tying your sling together, wondering how your life went so badly off track.

George sings "Finishing the Hat" in *Sunday in the Park with George* because he's going through his sketch book and comes across a sketch of Dot, who is looking for him to show off Louis, her new boyfriend.

The moment before is a pinch. It's an event that creates a sense of urgency in you, forces you to feel something and do something about it. It should make you feel alive from your head to your toes.

Again, the cyclical nature of this work means that your moment before can be tailored as a result of your "Facts and Questions," "given circumstances," and what you can infer from the script. Sometimes the circumstances themselves will be enough to enliven you and sometimes you'll need to engage your imagination, using substitutions and personalizations to deepen your connection to them.

Make the moment before as hot as you can for yourself. There's no room for casual choices in the theatre, but you can choose something that tickles your brain: stub your toe, spill your drink, smell something bad in your moment before and see how that changes you.

Research

As unlimited as our imaginations are, we still need touchstones to create a foundation and structure. Every piece is a period piece, whether it takes place in the 1890s or 2020. And we are all products of the period we inhabit. We are directly affected by the politics, entertainment, technology, fashion, and scientific advances that surround us. I'm not asking you to become a dramaturge, but it's very helpful to have more than a passing familiarity with the aspects I list above when performing. The fact that the adolescents in *Spring Awakening* pull out microphones for their songs is intentionally shocking, as mics didn't exist at the time. There are no telephones, let alone cell phones, in the world of *Hello, Dolly*. The characters in *The Wild Party* are products of the roaring twenties, defying Prohibition. It's integral for you to understand these circumstances by researching the time period in which the action is set.

Also included in research is looking up the meaning and pronunciation of any word you do not know or are not sure of. You can't act a word if you don't know what it means! Someone will know you're faking it. You have a computer literally at your fingertips (even though I asked you to put it in the other room or in airplane mode)—use it!

If you were cast in any role in *A Strange Loop* some topics of research would be as follows:

A STRANGE LOOP / RESEARCH ITEMS

Who is Michael R. Jackson, the composer/lyricist?

What else has he written?

Why did he write this?

Jackson quotes the Liz Phair song "Strange Loop" in the intro. Who is Liz Phair?

Listen to this song as well as the other "white girls" referenced.

What is a loop?

What makes it strange?

How is the "strange loop" reflected in the show?

What is the job of a Broadway usher?

Do ushers have relationships with the creatives and performers?

What are the perks of being an usher?

What are the challenges of being an usher?

What is an usher's pay?

Is it difficult to get a job as an usher?

Can you afford rent on an usher salary alone?

What's the average rent in Manhattan?

Do you have to have another job?

What neighborhoods in NYC do struggling young artists live?

The Lion King, movie vs. show: similarities and differences.

How long has the show been running?

What theatre is the show in?

How many people does it seat?

How many performances a week?

Who is the majority of the audience? Tourists? Children? Locals? Foreign?

How does one write a musical?

What's the percentage of Black musical theatre writers?

What's the percentage of working Black musical theatre writers?

What are the organizations and resources for Black musical theatre writers?

What's the process of getting a new musical produced?

What are the best schools for musical theatre writing?

How much does a degree cost?

Who is Tyler Perry?

What works are in his canon?

Research is meant to deepen and enrich your work. In order to create and live in the world of the show, you need to immerse yourself in it. This isn't method acting. It's homework. This isn't something you can fake. Working in a service job in a Broadway theatre in Times Square is a very specific job. Commuting home on the subway at ten o'clock at night after a long shift is a very specific experience. Living in New York City and trying to break into professional theatre while working a survival job is one of the most challenging experiences ever. Our individual experiences are directly influenced by our very specific circumstances.

When you're interpreting a real-life figure, it is helpful to know as much as possible about that person and the world they inhabited. Think of all the things that influence you on a daily basis (music, television, movies, podcasts, books, theatre, etc.) and find out what those influences could be or have been for your character. We are direct products of our circumstances, whether we embrace them or rebel against them. In real life, George Seurat of *Sunday in the Park with George* was rebelling against contemporary ideas of painting to create something new, but he understood what he was rebelling against.

Polarities

Polarities are opposing forces. *Beginning/end* are polarities, as are *happy/sad*, and *positive/negative*. I want you to mine the text for them. When you're working on a scene or a song, try to pinpoint where you end emotionally and then start the piece from the opposite place. The main event (remember that?) of the scene or the song will be the moment when this transition/realization/revelation occurs.

Ultimately, your entire journey during the show should be an opposition: you start in one place and end up in another one physically, spiritually, mentally, and emotionally. The Baker goes from a childless married man to a widower with a child in *Into the Woods*. Tracy goes from outcast rebel to leader in *Hairspray*. George goes from sketches to finished painting in the first act of *Sunday in the Park with George*, and then becomes a descendant of Seurat in act 2. Polarities generate good tension, internally and externally, and you should constantly be looking for them.

There are small but important ways to create them for yourself that are unseen by the audience but fill you emotionally as a performer. A simple but ingenious example of this happened when I was directing *Songbird*, a musical off-Broadway. The action took place in Nashville and was inspired by Anton Chekhov's *The Seagull*. One of the subplots was about an unmarried doctor having a long-term affair with a married bartender. After he comes to her house one afternoon to speak to her, the scene culminates in her ending the affair. He leaves, heartbroken. The actor playing Doc was always so emotionally full at the end of the scene, truly devastated. I complimented him on this moment, which was honest and painful to behold. He told me that he entered the scene with a wedding ring in his shirt pocket: he planned on proposing. He was going to ask the bartender to leave her husband and be with him. There was no textual support for this choice. No one, including me, knew that he crafted this. But it was imaginative, emotionally alive, and active. He made an informed choice based on his interpretation of the text and his character's objective. He set himself up, as an actor, for an amazing fall. Losses are great events to plan for our characters. The actor went into the scene with the intention of proposing and ended it heartbroken and alone.

If you're having difficulty defining your character upon the first few reads, you can use polarities to help you. Where do they end up? Put yourself in a different state at the beginning and try to pinpoint the moments of change—the main events. Or look around you at the other characters and create someone who is the opposite. This is an instance of using types—broad, seemingly stereotypical outlines—in order to get more specific.

In *Hairspray,* there are huge differences between Tracy and Penny. There are also huge differences between Tracy and Amber, and Amber and Penny. At a very simple level, Tracy is the go-getter, Penny is flighty, and Amber is the snob. It can be very helpful to start with these very basic archetypes and build from there. In *Spring Awakening*, you can look at Melchior as the brain, or the teacher, and Moritz as the student. Wendla is civilized and contained in opposition to Ilse's free spirit. In *Caroline, or Change*, Caroline is a boiling pot with the lid on and Emmie, her daughter, has no lid—she's erupting. In *Hello, Dolly* you can see this in Cornelius and Barnaby as well as Irene and Minnie. These four roles are typically cast with contrasting physical types as well to highlight the differences. Look for and create polarities everywhere.

Language and Rhythm

Every great work has its own sound, its own rhythm. Every character has their own way of communicating, their own sound. Some musicals even have a unique language. *Wicked* has words like "confusifying," "definish," and "degreenify." *West Side Story* has phrases created by book writer Arthur Laurents like "rig a tum tum." In *West Side Story* this language also allows the characters to curse without there being actual profanity in the book. This language needs to sound natural coming out of your mouth, and so you will probably need to spend some time saying "rig a tum tum" in different situations and in different ways to define what it means to you.

Acting "on the line" will help you find the rhythm of the piece. If you keep breaking the line apart, you'll never find the flow. Shakespeare is the king of language and rhythm. It can be intimidating to tackle his work, but all of his characters think and talk differently, and this is sculpted within by the actual language. Romeo speaks differently from Juliet, who speaks differently from the Nurse, whose language is unlike anyone else's in the play. In my experience, musical theatre actors excel at Shakespeare because they understand rhythm.

To bring it back to musical theatre, Moritz speaks differently from Melchior. Tracy speaks differently from Penny. Roxy speaks differently from Velma, and so on. Leaning into the rhythm of your character will help you shape and mold them. Acting on the line and honoring the punctuation (as discussed in the "Actions" section) will help reveal the rhythm of the language and the character.

Playlist

Like your vision board, create a playlist of music to get you into the world or mood of the show. You can use music from the show, music from the period, and music that makes you think about the character or their emotional life. It's only for you, so let loose!

Trust and Play

I do believe all of this work is necessary. I practice it myself. It will allow you to understand your character and the world of the play, ultimately, on an instinctual level, the impulses of your character.

Once you get into rehearsal, the true challenge becomes letting the work go and allowing yourself to play, experience, and discover. Trust yourself. Trust your partners. Trust your collaborators. Focus not on yourself but on everything around you. How are you affecting and being affected by the stimuli around you? Stay flexible and open to change.

You can come back to this work when you're struggling or stuck over a moment, a scene, or a relationship. Reexamine your objectives. Switch up your actions. Refine your given circumstances. Then, jump back in.

Auditions

All of the work I've described above is enormously helpful once you've been cast in a show. However, it's also very useful for auditions, whether scheduled auditions or cold readings.

In a scheduled audition, I would work on the following items:

1. Objectives
2. Given Circumstances
3. World of the Show
4. Main Event
5. Similarities and Differences

6. Relationships
7. Actions
8. Atmosphere
9. The Moment Before
10. Polarities
11. Language and Rhythm

In a cold reading, if you have about five to ten minutes to prepare, work on these:

1. Objective
2. Relationships
3. Atmosphere

You simply can't act without an objective. Your character needs something. They're fighting for something. The objective keeps you moving forward and active.

Conclusion

Vivid storytelling requires an understanding of structure, an emotional connection to the character you're playing, and an active objective. All of the exercises outlined above are in the service of making you a more specific storyteller with a deep understanding of the text. It's fairly simple to memorize your lines and say them however you feel in the moment, unrehearsed and unprepared. You will work with creative teams that are very hands-on and creative teams that never give you a single note. At the end of the day, you are responsible for what you put on stage. If you want to call yourself an artist, if you care about your work, whether you're getting paid or not, you want to work to the best of your potential. These exercises will help you get there.

Act III

THE SCORE

"Listen to the music, music doesn't lie."

—Michael John LaChuisa

Score Work

Now that you've done a thorough investigation of the text, it's time to take a look at the score. Composers take just as much time crafting the music as the book writer does the libretto. Therefore, equal attention needs to be paid here.

Along with everything covered previously in this book, you now have to add another layer of storytelling that incorporates your voice and your body in a heightened state. I'm going to start off by saying something you might not want to hear: It's not about how high you can sing. It's not about how loud you can sing. It's not about how well you riff. It's not even about how perfect you sound.

Great musical theatre performances are so much more than vocal acrobatics. Great musical theatre performances are about storytelling. Idina Menzel didn't win a Tony Award for *Wicked* just because she belted the hell out of "Defying Gravity." Of course, that specific moment requires vocal heft and power, but if the whole role was performed at that level, her voice wouldn't have survived eight shows a week. More importantly, the audience would grow aurally bored of hearing the same sound at the same level for two and a half hours. Knowing this, Idina and the creative team leaned into the quiet sadness of "I'm Not That Girl," the unsettling disquiet of "Something Bad," and the loving tenderness of "For Good." (Polarities!) These dynamics are necessary to tell the story and keep the audience engaged.

Some of our most treasured stars are revered not for their vocal range but for their unique vocal qualities. Performers like Harvey Fierstein, Nathan Lane, Audra McDonald, and Bernadette Peters are gifted storytellers and song interpreters.

Musical theatre needs all types; the basses, baritones, and altos of the world are just as impressive as other performers when paired with great storytelling. Your goal should be a fully developed, nuanced performance.

When you're in doubt, or feeling the need to push, please go back to the first section of this book and remember who you are and who you want to be. You are and always will be enough. There is freedom to explore the depth and range of your voice.

Types of Musical Theatre Songs

Whether up-tempo songs or slow ballads, every song in a musical has a specific function. It's helpful as the storyteller to know what the narrative function of the song is in the construction of the musical. The following, listed alphabetically, are some of the more common types of musical theatre songs to be familiar with:

11 O'clock Number: So named because curtain used to go up at 8:30 p.m., and this penultimate number would arrive around 11 p.m. This type of song, sung by the leading character, usually makes an important decision causing an important turn in the action.

Action Song: A song that moves the plot forward.

Entr'acte: An instrumental piece that opens act 2; an abbreviated overture.

Finale: The number that wraps up all the loose ends and relays the message or moral of the story.

"I Am" / Character / Charm Song: This type of song may incorporate the objective but, instead of moving the action forward, the action for all intents and purposes stops while the character tells us who they are.

"I Want" Song: One that introduces the main character and defines what their objective is.

Opening Number: A song that introduces the world of the show, identifies the leading and supporting characters, and establishes style and tone.

Overture: The instrumental introduction to the show, usually highlighting songs the audience will hear throughout the performance.

Production Number: A number incorporating song and dance with the entire (or nearly entire) cast.

Reprise: A repetition of a song introduced earlier in the show, usually shows a moment of growth or reflection when revisited.

Soliloquy: A song in which a character expresses their thoughts and feelings aloud either to themselves or—my preference—to the audience. Soliloquies need forward movement when performed. Keep your objective and actions in mind. If you get too reflective, the song becomes inactive.

The Composition

Our job as storytellers is to honor the writer. You would not make up your own lines of dialogue. Therefore, you shouldn't change the composition without specific permission from the writer or the musical director.

A general rule of life is this: know the rules before you break them. So even if you're given permission to change the musicality of the piece, it's necessary to understand how it was first written and the circumstances around the placement in the show.

It is imperative that you understand the following:

- the key in which the song is written
- the tempo the composer wrote the number in
- any articulations the composer has notated
- any key changes, known as modulations, within the song
- note-values: whole, half, quarter, etc. (If you think there isn't a difference between a quarter note and a

half note, think of the difference between an "a" and a "the" in a sentence.)

- rests

A basic knowledge of music theory beyond the above is imperative for any performer. It's worth researching courses in your area or online.

Musicality

Musicality is *how* you sing. Once you've learned the structure of the song, I want you to focus on the following:

- Pitch
- Tone
- Placement
- Phrasing
- Dynamics
- Diction
- Synthesis

Pitch or intonation is the high or low frequency of a sound. When you sing, it's the speed at which your vocal chords are vibrating. Think of it as the acoustic sound you produce and hear.

Tone is the quality with which you are singing: warm, light, dark, heavy, and so on.

Placement is quite literally where in your body you feel the resonance of the sound you're producing. Tone and placement go hand in hand.

Phrasing is the way in which you sing the song, honoring the composition and following the punctuation in the lyrics. Trust the writers.

(WARNING: Do you remember in the "Script" section when I wrote about acting on the line? "Back phrasing"—delaying a word in a lyric beyond its expected beat—is akin to singing off the line. Sometimes it can be used to create tension, but in most cases I find it does nothing but destroy the musicality the composer intended. Use back phrasing cautiously and intentionally—if at all.)

Dynamics refers to controlling your volume when you sing. It's a very useful tool in creating tension as well as control. You don't want a song—or even a sixteen-bar cut—to sit at the same dynamic the entire time. In learning how to judge the dynamics of any given space, think about your voice hitting the back wall in whichever direction you are facing. That is the maximum amount of volume you need to hit. Dynamics and phrasing work hand in hand in showing your artistry.

Diction is the clarity of your pronunciation. I like to think that vowels are the sound our hearts make, while consonants give those feelings form and meaning. It's imperative that you shape the sounds you are speaking and singing. Basic storytelling is about language. We often can be lazy in our everyday speech, but we can't afford that when performing.

Synthesis is putting all of these elements together. A great voice teacher will help you achieve synthesis.

Lose the Lyrics

At this stage of the process, I find it helpful to put the words aside and listen to what the music is telling me. Take the following cut of "I Dreamed a Dream" from *Les Miserables*. Notice how the descending notes mimic Fantine's emotional descent into a dark place. You can practically feel the sounds rumbling in your gut. This is a person who has lost something important, who has been deeply wounded by life. Then she swoops up into an almost primal scream.

Now, marry the lyrics to the music and see how they support each other.

Notice the imagery that causes Fantine to take that dive into the depths and how the word "shame" is what causes the scream.

Finally, if there are recorded versions of a given song, I highly suggest you listen—not to the recorded vocals, but to the orchestrations. Orchestrators are major collaborators, especially on original productions of a show. The sound that they're creating is reinforcing the intention of the creative team.

Monologue the Song

Here is where you apply the tools from "Act II" of this book:

- Super Objective
- Scene Objective
- Song Objective
- Given Circumstances
- World of the Show
- Main Event
- Relationships
- Actions
- Atmosphere
- The Moment Before
- Polarities

Let's proceed with "I Dreamed a Dream" for a moment, a song that can be considered a character song or a soliloquy.

In terms of the **Given Circumstances**, we know the following:

- My name is Fantine.
- I live in Montreuil-sur-Mer, France.
- The year is approximately 1821.
- I have a child named Cosette.
- Cosette lives with the Thernardiers, and I send money to them.
- I have no husband, and the father of the child abandoned me.
- I have just been fired.
- Without money, I can't pay for food, shelter, or Cosette's care.

The **Main Event** of the song happens around "So different now from what it seemed," when Fantine realizes that hope for a happy family life is gone.

Lyrics, just like lines of dialogue, can also be rendered as **Actions**. For example,

"There was a time when men were kind"—to rouse

"When their voices were soft"—to touch

"And their words inviting"—to open

. . .

"There was a time / It all went wrong"—to confess

The **Atmosphere** for the song is dark, heavy, oppressive.

Fantine's **Moment Before** the song is her having just been fired.

Polarities: The performer may rouse up the memory of a better, happier, hopeful time in order to quell the fear, but by the end of the song they give up dreaming and decide to do what must be done, no matter how difficult, demeaning, or degrading.

You would then continue to do this for every song in the show. In Fantine's case, "Lovely Ladies" and her descent into sex work comes next.

Conclusion

A great musical theatre performer understands how to marry the words and the music. In order to do this, it's helpful to approach and study them separately before beginning the process of putting them together. Each note, each phrase means as much as a word and a thought. The music tells the story of your character hand in hand with the book. Allow yourself the patience and time to dissect all the elements thoughtfully, precisely, and with specificity so that you're making deliberate, informed choices when interpreting the material.

Act IV

ETIQUETTE

"Etiquette means behaving yourself a little better than is absolutely essential."

—Will Cuppy

Production Behavior

I've learned in my time that there are a lot of unspoken rules about how and how not to behave during all aspects of a musical theatre production. As someone who is usually more socially awkward than not, I find the following advice very helpful on a personal level. I find, as I'm sure you know by now, having a set guideline to follow incredibly useful.

While most training programs focus on the art and craft aspects of the work, I find they tend to neglect etiquette and behavior, assuming you'll learn it in class and in productions. But let's be honest: there's never enough time in a class or production to focus on these aspects; there's work to be done.

I've compiled the following list to speak some of the unspoken "rules" that will help you throughout a production. After all, so much of this business is about word of mouth. Along with your talent and craft, you want to be someone people want to work with. You want to be someone that creatives want in a room. You want to be a team player. Hopefully, this guide will help.

I try to phrase things as positively as possible, but I'm afraid you're going to find a lot of "don't" statements in the following. Stephen Sondheim was right, apparently: everybody says "don't."

The First Day of Rehearsal

- Assume everyone is as excited and as nervous as you.
- Do not isolate yourself.
- Approach individuals and introduce yourself.
- Tell them what your role is (even if you're an understudy or a swing).
- Make conversation by asking questions, not talking about yourself.
- Seek out the director, producer, and casting director and thank them for the opportunity.

Appropriate Dress

- Dress in a silhouette similar to your character:
  - If your character wears long pants, do not rehearse in shorts.
  - If your character wears a skirt, wear a skirt.
- You should be able to move in these clothes, as your character would move.

- Do not wear clothing with logos printed on them. You want your partner focusing on you, your face, your body, and your behavior—*not* reading your T-shirt or laughing at the funny print or slogan on it.

- Do not wear open-toed shoes or sandals—ever—unless the role requires them. Do not *ever* rehearse a fight scene in open-toed shoes.

- Do not change your hair length, color, or style at any time before rehearsal starts or during the process without consulting your director or designer first.

Personal Hygiene

- Brush your teeth before every rehearsal and after every break, especially after eating or smoking.

- Shower every day and before every performance.

- Wear clean clothes to rehearsal every day. If you wear the same things, figure out a way to wash them as much as possible.

- Go to the gym, do yoga, meditate. Eight shows a week require strength and stamina. Film shoots can be long and exhausting.

- Get seven to eight hours of sleep a night.

- Drink and smoke in moderation, if at all.

From the First Read-Through to Rehearsals

- Bring a pencil and paper with you—every day. Have backups.

- Have a notebook that is solely for the show you are working on. This notebook contains things like this:
  - Character thoughts (your own and your character's thoughts on other characters in the play)
  - Facts about the play
  - Facts about your character
  - What other characters say about you
  - The given circumstances for every scene
  - Questions
  - Daydreams
  - Notes from the director

- Phones are not a place to take notes at any time during the process.

- Do not "remember" notes. Write them down, by hand, in your notebook. The process of writing aids your memory.

- Character Idea: Have one based on an intelligent reading and analysis of the script. Your character idea should be flexible.

- ○ The director may steer you in a different direction. Try it for a few days.
- ○ If it doesn't feel right, explain why, and use your reading and analysis of the script to support your case.
- ○ Don't be defensive with your director. It's a collaboration.
- ○ Ultimately, your director has the final say.

- Don't highlight your lines during the read-through. *Listen* to the play.

- Don't look ahead to see when you're next on stage. *Listen* to the play.

- Don't emphasize pronouns. These are very often the least interesting words in the sentence.

- Do take in your scene partner(s) during the first read and respond to what they're doing. The script will always be there. Your initial instincts and impulses won't be.

- Don't be late.
  - ○ Give yourself time to arrive at least ten minutes early.
  - ○ You should be ready to work at start time, not arriving.
  - ○ If you need time to warm up, factor this into your travel time.

- *Listen.* Listen to everyone.
  - Pay attention to what the director says about the world of the play.
  - Even if it does not immediately give you information about your character, specifically, he or she is sharing their vision of the show with you.
  - You can very often pick up something valuable to use immediately or in the future as you create your character. This information informs your choices.
- Don't ask too many questions right away.
- Don't make everything about you or your character.
- The rehearsal process is one of discovery and you shouldn't discover everything in the first week. Also, if you *listen* you may discover the answer to your questions without having to ask.
- Look up the definition and pronunciation of any word or reference you do not know.
- Once you're up on your feet, find an activity for every scene you're in.
  - We rarely sit and talk. Activity creates behavior.
  - Physical activities help ground us in the scene and the world of the play.

- Don't confuse your *fear* with your *process*. It is your job to take risks in rehearsal and this doesn't always happen in your comfort zone or when you are ready to.

- Don't use the word "process" to defend your insecurities.

- Unless otherwise instructed, be off-book the second time you get to a scene.

- Use the rehearsal room as your opportunity to *TAKE CHANCES*.

- Don't stand in your own way. Listen to the script and your director, not your ego.

- Don't enter a scene to "have a scene" with your partner.
  - Come in with an objective.
  - It's your job to keep that person in the room and vice versa.

- Always find a sense of urgency in your character.

- Always find a sense of humor in your character.

- Come back from breaks on time and ready to work.

- Respect the work of your fellow actors.
  - Don't talk while they're working.
  - Don't text/email while they're working.
  - Don't eat noisy/smelly food while they're working.

- Ask the stage manager if you can leave the room if you're not being used and don't want to watch.
- Be respectful and quiet outside of the room if you know that you can be heard inside.
- Be patient if you're sitting around and waiting to work.
- You want the director to take as much time with you as they are taking with your fellow cast mates.
- Talk to your partner about consent and boundaries
  - Don't touch, kiss, slap, or hit them in any way without speaking to them about it first.
  - Try not to paraphrase lines.
  - Keep the lines of communication open at all times.
  - No matter what the size of your role is, you are part of a bigger picture.
- You are almost always replaceable. Keep your ego in check.

Tech, Performances, and Notes

- Stage managers and their assistants have the hardest jobs in the world.
  - Listen to them.
  - Respect them.
  - Appreciate them.

- Tech is a time to put everything together. Use that time on stage to run lines, work scenes, get comfortable in the space.
  - Acoustics in every house are different. Run lines with your scene partners with one of you on stage, one of you in the back of the house so that you get an idea of how much work you need to fill the space.
  - Do not rely on microphones to do the work for you. You still need vocal energy and support in order to tell the story.
  - Tech hours are long and tedious, pace yourself and get lots of rest.
  - Do not wear white for tech.
  - Do not wear hats or caps that cover your eyes or any part of your face in tech.
  - Do not go out and drink and party during tech.
  - Make friends with all the tech people working backstage and in the house. Thank them for what they do.
  - Make friends with the ushers.
  - Everyone is there with one goal in mind, making great theatre.
  - Tech is probably not the best time to ask your director major character questions. His/her focus is most likely elsewhere but will return to you shortly.

- Don't fall in love with any costume, set, prop, or hairstyle because it's all subject to change.
- Changes made to the above are not about *you* but about the visual storytelling of the show.
- Note sessions are not the time for you to privately discuss the performance with your cast mates while the director gives note.
  - Have your notepad and pen for notes.
  - Listen to what the director is saying, to other people and you.
  - Write down the notes whether they be big, small, or in between.

Previews

Previews take their toll on everyone.

- The creatives are making changes based on audience response.
- No one is working more or less hard than anyone else.
- You're rehearsing all day and performing at night.
- Sleep in if you need to sleep in. Eat healthy. Pace yourself.
- Be patient.
- Grant grace.

- Your favorite moment might get cut in the interest of storytelling. It's not personal.
- The bad mood of one person can affect the entire company. Try not to be that one person.
- Communicate. Communicate Communicate. Are there safety issues? Are there issues you can see and fix without making an announcement?
- Be a problem solver.

The Run

- The creative team departs, leaving the stage manager and associates in charge.
- All questions, concerns, and issues go through the stage manager, who will be in constant contact with the creative team.
- The stage manager and associates are charged with maintaining the integrity of the production and, as such, can give notes.
- Every performance is a new audience who has never experienced the show before; try to see your performances through their eyes.

Finale

"In the end, we'll all become stories."

—Margaret Atwood

The work of a storyteller is never-ending. Once you've done the analysis, the rehearsal, and the tech, then you're in performance mode, running the show regularly. It's your job to faithfully represent what's been created while still keeping your performance fresh. The best way to keep it fresh is to clear your mind, stay alert, and listen. Fight the urge to allow autopilot to take over. Remember you have the power to influence and change one person's life in the audience—and probably more than that.

Building and maintaining a life in the theatre takes a lot of work. I hope you embrace that work fully with an open heart and an open mind, all the while retaining the childlike wonder you had upon experiencing your first show.

It will not be easy. There will be periods of too much work. There will be periods of no work. You'll want to give up. You'll want to become cynical and maybe even a little bitter. Fight these feelings! Remember, right here, right now, I'm telling you it will be a challenge. But don't let anyone tell you to give it up. In those dry periods, pull out a script for a show you love and do this work. We stay inspired and creative through doing, not through waiting.

That ten-year-old boy whose life changed in the Gershwin Theatre all those years ago is in his fifth decade in life and his third decade as an industry professional. I still approach every show I'm about to see as if it's going to change my life. I don't worry about the performers anymore because I know how hard they've worked and how excited they are to share that work with an audience. Sometimes I'm transported. Sometimes I'm disappointed. There are weeks when I'll see a show a day; other times, weeks will pass with no show at all. But I never take this for granted.

Justin Guarini and I got to open a show on Broadway. How cool is that? It was one of the greatest experiences of my life. I think about it every day. Beyond that, I get to go into a classroom every week and share what I've learned with the next generation of artists who will go on to change the theatrical world, onstage and off. Ten-year-old me would never have believed it—fortysomething me still can't. And that's the magic and wonder of theatre. Anyone can do it.

I hope you remember there's no one like you.

I hope you love to tell stories.

I hope you realize the power that you have inside of you to change the world.

I hope this is a book you'll come back to throughout your career for guidance and inspiration.

I hope you'll remember that the road you're on is different from anyone else's.

I hope you'll trust that and have faith in yourself.

I hope you see yourself as an artist as well as a craftsperson.

I hope you'll laugh a lot and make lifelong friends.

I hope you won't take a moment for granted, inside a theatre or out.

I hope we get to work together one day.

I hope to see you on stage.

Glossary

The following is an abbreviated list of people, words, and phrases you'll come across in your journey through this book and beyond.

10 out of 12: A rehearsal day during tech in which performers are called for a full twelve hours and work ten of them, that is, noon to midnight.

Actors' Equity Association: The union representing actors and stage managers. AEA supports its members by negotiating wages, improving working conditions, as well as providing health benefits and pension plans. AEA replaced its former EMC (Equity Membership Candidate) Program (in which an actor could accrue a number of points by working with participating theatres across the country) with its Open Access Program. See their website for details.

Agent: A representative for the actor who helps them obtain auditions and negotiate contracts. Traditionally, an agent receives about 10 percent to 15 percent of a performer's pay.

Book/Book Writer (also called Libretto): The book is the narrative structure of the musical, usually but not always including dialogue, that pieces the story together from beginning to end. Even musicals such as *Contact* and *Movin' Out*, which had no dialogue, had the structure credited to a book writer.

Broadway: Located in Manhattan's Theater District, there are currently forty-one Broadway houses that range in size from 500 to 1,900 (the Gershwin), a geographical area from 41st Street to 61st Street.

Casting Director: The casting director schedules auditions and chooses which performers are brought in to see the creative team. They are responsible for making the initial offers and arranging contact between the performer and management.

Choreographer: Working in tandem with the director, they are responsible for all dance and movement throughout the course of a show. Their job is to tell the story through movement.

Commercial Theatre: Theatre produced with the intention of making a profit for its investors.

Company Manager: The liaison between the performer and upper management. They are generally in charge of box office payroll, lodging, transportation, and the daily administrative operations of a show.

Composer: The writer of the music.

Costume Designer: The person responsible for telling the story through the clothing that the performer wears, usually identifying and defining character through color, pattern, and style.

Crew: The people working in various technical departments backstage from load-in through closing/load-out. They are in charge of every facet of the day-to-day technical running of the show from behind the scenes.

Dance Captain: A member of the company who is charged with maintaining the choreography during the run of the show. The dance captain knows every track and will often "swing out" (watch the show during a performance from the audience) to note the show and preserve the integrity of the physical storytelling. They will also often rehearse new company members into the show. This responsibility comes with a pay increase.

Dialect Coach: The person responsible for aiding all company members with any voice and speech work, specifically dialect, accents, and regionalisms.

Director: The person who oversees all the creative elements of a production and provides guidance to each individual department in an effort to achieve a cohesive production.

Dramaturge: A researcher and editor who assists with the quality and accuracy of a script.

Equity Principal Audition: A show-specific, all-day casting call in which members of the creative team must be present to audition AEA performers, whether they have an agent or not. Performers can come first thing in the morning, sign up for an appointment time, and return at said time with the guarantee of being seen. The focus of the EPA is on leading and supporting roles. EPAs are required for both musicals and plays. Performers are asked to perform a thirty-two-bar cut for the musical portion of these auditions. You can sign up online and you must show up twenty minutes before your time slot.

Equity Chorus Call: Similar to the EPA but focusing on ensemble members for musicals. Traditionally the ECC is split up into a dancers' call and a singers' call. In the dancers' call, a large group is usually taught the entire combination at once and then performs it in a smaller group. In a singers' call, performers are allotted sixteen bars. You can sign up online and you must show up thirty minutes before the start of the call.

Fight Coordinator: The person working with the director and actors to safely, theatrically, and effectively stage all fights.

General Manager: The person or persons who work directly with the producer to oversee budget, timeline, and hiring for all departments, as well as manage day-to-day operations of a production.

Intimacy Coordinator: The person working with the director and actors to stage any moments that require physical and/or emotional vulnerability.

Invited Dress: The dress/tech rehearsal, usually before the first public performance, to which friends and family of the company and crew are invited free of charge.

Libretto: *See* Book/Book Writer

Lighting Designer: The person responsible for focusing the story, mood, character, and architecture through light.

Lyricist: The person who writes the words that accompany the music.

Make-Up Design: The person responsible for any make-up requirements from basic looks to special effects.

Manager: Similar to an agent, a manager is acting as a representative of a performer. Managers usually have a smaller client base, take on a more advisory role, and also take a bigger percentage of a performer's salary (typically 15–25 percent).

Music Director: The person responsible for all musical elements of a show including teaching music to the company, rehearsing the orchestra, and conducting performances.

Musical Contractor: The person responsible for hiring, coordinating, and contracting musicians.

Not-for-Profit Theatre: A company that receives government funding and also receives revenue from memberships, rentals, and fund raising. All of the profits go directly back into the company. There are four major nonprofits producing on Broadway: Lincoln Center, Manhattan Theatre Club, Roundabout Theatre Company, and Second Stage.

Off-Broadway: Smaller than a Broadway theatre and in a less concentrated area, these houses seat between 100 and 499 patrons.

Open Call: An audition available to both union and non-union performers.

Orchestra: The musicians who play the score during a performance.

Orchestrator: The person working alongside the composer to select the instrumentation and create the musical score for all of the instruments in the orchestra.

Previews: The period of time prior to opening when a show is performing for a paying audience but still rehearsing and making changes during the day.

Producer: The big boss! They are the creative and business head of the entire production and have final say on all aspects.

Production Assistant: The person who assists the stage management team in printing and distributing scripts, running errands, and other aspects of rehearsal and production as needed.

Projection Designer: A member of the creative team who creates and integrates film and other graphic elements into the other physical elements of the design.

Production Stage Manager: Head of stage management team on large shows, the PSM oversees all the practical technical aspects of running the show as well as the day-to-day minutiae.

Props Manager: A craftsperson and artist who sources, designs, and builds the props and set pieces.

Put-In: A rehearsal in which a new company member, a swing, an understudy, or a stand-by is given the opportunity to go through their entire track with the entire company.

Regional Theater: A professional theatre company usually located outside of New York City and usally nonprofit.

Resident Director: The right hand of the director, and responsible for maintaining the artistic integrity of the production after opening as well as rehearsing new cast members into the show.

Score: The written form of the vocal and orchestral musical parts.

Society of Stage Directors and Choreographers: The union for directors and choreographers.

Scenic Designer: The person responsible for creating the physical architecture of the playing space.

GLOSSARY

Sound Designer: The person responsible for all auditory elements of a production from sound mixing to effects.

Stand-By: An off-stage cast member whose job is to cover leading/supporting roles and literally "stand-by" in case they are called upon to go on.

Swing: An off-stage cast member who is responsible for learning a number of ensemble tracks.

Technical Rehearsals: Otherwise known as "tech," the period of times when the production moves into the theatre and all design elements are put together in preparation for the first performance.

Theatre Owner: The business that owns, operates, and rents theatres for a production. The major theatre owners on Broadway are ATG/Jujamcyn, the Nederlander Organization, and the Shubert Organization.

Track: The physical map a performer has over the course of a performance including dialogue, vocal parts, and choreography.

Understudy: A member of the cast usually in a featured or ensemble role who must learn the part of a leading or supporting player. When the understudy goes on, a swing goes on in their track.

Universal Swing: A cast member that is hired to cover roles in *all* running companies of a show: Broadway, First National Tour, sit-down productions, and so on.

Vocal Arranger: A member of the music team who creates the combination of vocal parts for the company.

Wig/Hair Designer: The person responsible for the physical composition of all hair needs.

Acknowledgments

I am forever indebted to Justin Guarini for his friendship, support, humor, and truth.

Thanks to Susan Bristow, Jim Carnahan, Katya Campbell, Felicia Curry, Erin Dilly, Edward Fagley, Eric Gelb, Allen Gorney, Gabriela Hernandez, Cory Jeacoma, Jane Lew, David Leveaux, Abby Linderman, Conor McShane, Michael Mayer, Tom McVey, Amy Saltz, Jael Scott, Calvin Leon Smith, Leroy Thompson, Alexander Tom, and Madison Willett for influencing and advising on this journey.

Thanks to all my students over the years, for giving me space to fail and to play, and for teaching me more than I teach them.

Chris Chappell and his team at Applause Books helped grow this book from the seed of an idea through full development.

ACKNOWLEDGMENTS

This book could not have been completed without the assistance of Pace University's Book and Performance Completion Award.

Special thanks to my parents for igniting and stoking the fire. And, as always, to Joe—for a home.

Index